Seer

JOHN THOMSON

The words within the pages that follow are dedicated to the Truth of a very special woman…

Ave Maria…Salve Regina…

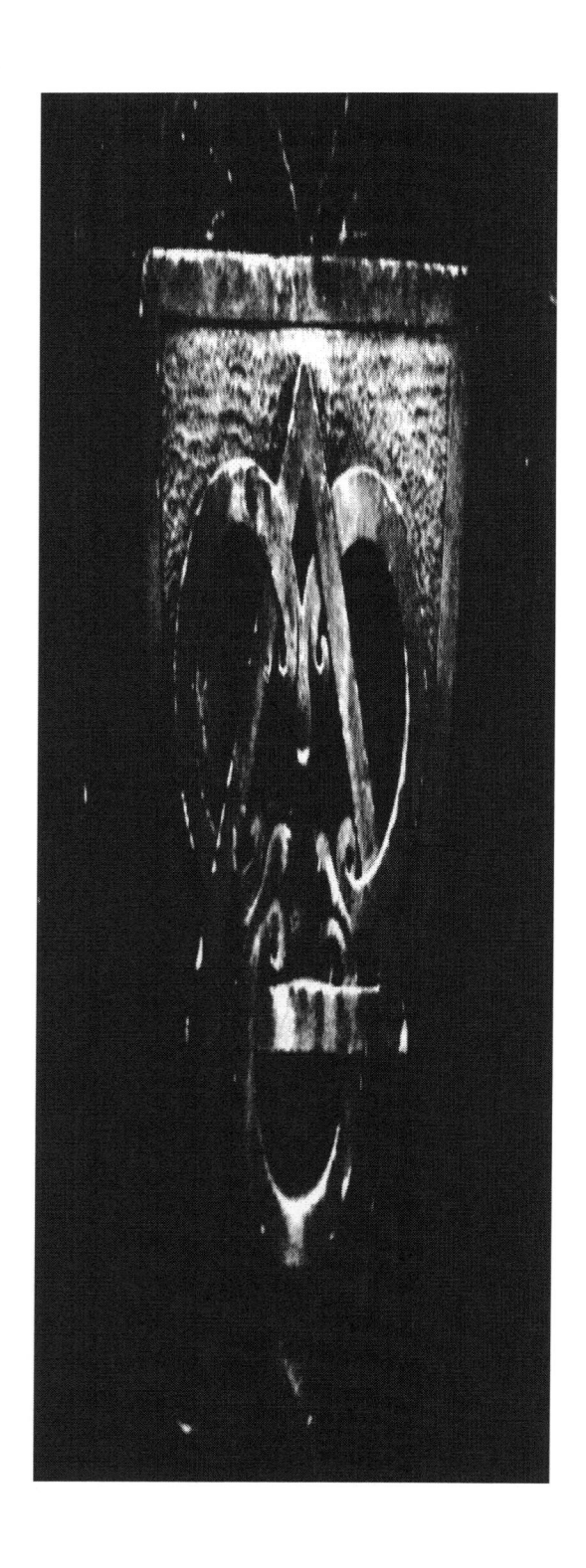

'Manila comes for you…'

6 August 2012

I couldn't have known...

How could I have possibly known that this was to happen for me? There's no way I could've known...

But when I look back at the man I was before this beautiful experience awakened within and around me...it seems I may have known something very important was about to happen and that somehow I would be part of it. But there's no way I could've known that it would centre around me...the very essence of who and what I am...

How could I have known I was to be blessed with a beautiful gift? A gift so gentle and so powerful...something I believe to be a blessing. Me...a man of no religion...

But I am a man of faith. My faith is the humanity within humankind...the precious truth of the magic which dwells within each and every one of us. That is my faith. A faith I was to find...a faith I was to see following a gentle and powerful experience which held me close in love during a time of my own darkness...

A part of me awakened that day...a part of me so very deep within. And if this magic is within me...then it must be within you too. Gentle...powerful...something I believe is the truth of all of us...

Something beautiful opened my eyes on that day...that sunny late summer day on England's west coast. And I had no idea of how important this experience was to become in my new life and my recovery from alcoholism. I couldn't have known. I couldn't have known that I was about to awaken to my gift of clairvoyance at the age of forty-two...in a place of healing...a last resort to somehow find hope in my life after losing everyone and everything as a result of my drinking...

My experience so gentle…my experience so powerful…was to take place in a treatment centre for addiction in September 2010.

This new vision was to play an integral part in my abstinence and it was to develop to such an extent that here were times when it overwhelmed me completely…sometimes seeing me on my knees in awe of what I was actually experiencing. Yet all of the time I knew I was being held safely by love and that no harm would come to me…

Much was to happen following that day so beautiful in 2010…so much I wish to share with you in the hope that it will help to see that hope can be found…even when all that can be seen is hopeless…

But first we need to go forward in time…

Manila comes for you…

Four words…four words which were to become evidence of my gift…

Manila comes for you…

Four words so simple…four words I'd seen appear before me one day in the late of summer 2012…

Manila comes for you…

For so long I'd been sharing with others of what I was experiencing…an experience for which I had no evidence…an experience which continues to this day…an experience which sees me receive messages from light so white…an experience which sees me shown information about events before they happen…

Manila comes for you…

The vision had taken place on the morning of 6 August 2012 on the east coast of England. The vision came from an essence of somewhere so beautiful…so powerful…so forgiving…so loving…

Manila comes for you…

The words appeared before me and so I did what I'd been doing for nearly a year...I texted the words to myself on my mobile phone. Four simple words...

Manila comes for you...

Later that day...the storm hit the Philippines...

Manila comes for you...

Typhoon Haikui hit the Philippines on the evening of 6 August 2012. I'd seen the words appear before me only several hours before the storm descended on Manila...words which I'd sent to myself by text on my mobile phone...

I'd seen information regarding a natural disaster...information regarding an event before it had happened. And this wasn't the first time...

My name is John and I live in Bristol…

It's here on the west coast of England where my experience began…where my experience continues…

What comes in the pages ahead is the Truth of how this all began for me…

I'm just an ordinary man…an ordinary man having an extraordinary experience…an experience which began when I surrendered to being an alcoholic and asked something unseen for help…when I offered myself with total honesty to a life that would help others…

My whole life changed from that moment on. My whole life was to receive a new purpose. And my new calling was to help others who suffer…as well as find the truth of a woman of beauty who lived so long ago…a woman whose truth I was to eventually see…a woman who was to guide me towards the man I am today…

What comes is my story…a story of Hope…a story of Truth…

Chapter One

The Message...

I want to be a good man for the rest of my life….

I know that I am a good man...deep within...an essence of light that shines not only from deep inside of me...but deep within us all. I know this to be true...

The truth is that I've seen a message...a message for me...and a message for you…

A truth so beautiful...so loving...so forgiving. A truth that has steered and guided me from a life in darkness...into a life of hope...

There have been many times over the past months...times when I've explained my experiences to others...only to be met by looks of confusion...looks of concern…

Fear has no place in the message that I've been shown...fear is removed once the message has been embraced…

Simplicity is the key for me to unlock for you and understanding of what I've been shown...a vision of hope...not just for me...for anyone who is willing to see…

I'm not a religious man...I do respect religion as organised faith helps those who suffer...answers to prayers. And that is a good thing…

Not religious...but with faith...I've always believed in something far greater than me...an essence of something that guides and loves me...loves us all...

This essence is my faith...this faith is what I see...I see the unseen and what I see is love. A vision so beautiful and pure...a new sight that opened my eyes to me and to life. The unseen became clear when I embraced honesty...my own truth...and it's this honesty that is the foundation of my recovery from alcohol...the keystone of my life...

So I'm going to keep this simple…

I wish to share my story with you in the hope that it will help you…if you need to find solace in your life…a comfort that I now find as I continue on my path…my journey in this world…

My name is John and I'm an alcoholic in recovery…chronic in the final years of my active addiction…and without hope in this world. I was hopeless and lost…filled with fear…and my will to live had gone. That was over two years ago…

The following truth of me is about how honesty embraced me…saved my life…and gave me a new vision of the world…a vision beyond my wildest dreams…a life beyond my wildest dreams…

This beautiful change has happened and continues to happen for me…and I believe that this beautiful change can happen for anyone. I walked through the doors of a rehabilitation centre in August 2010…lost and alone. It was there…in that *Place of Miracles*…that I found love…and where love found me…

I departed this special place five months later…blessed with a new hope for myself and blessed with a special gift. But I don't consider myself to be special…

The message of love and forgiveness found me in *The Place of Miracles*…guided me towards peace…opened my eyes…and gently steered me towards the truth of me…

I'd found a new vision of life in light. But first I'd had to face my own darkness…

Chapter Two

The Day Hope Came...

I spent years in my own darkness…

My beautiful encounter with Mary took place eleven months after my darkest hour…

It was early morning…7 June 2010…I awoke at 3am…

I was lying in a filthy bed in a single room in a homeless hostel on the east coast of England…

The town was Ipswich and my surroundings were a far cry from the lavish home that I once owned north of the border in Scotland…

The bed was filthy because I was filthy…

Covered in my own vomit and urine…I was a stinking mess…lying on top of the bed wearing only a pair of ripped and soaked combat trousers which I'd been wearing for days…

I could barely breath…

My tongue was swollen stiff and dry…gasping for air…craving fluids…I was so dehydrated…

Barely able to stand…I made it to the dirty sink and drank from the tap…I could feel life seeping back into me…and then the craving started…the panic began. It was early morning…nowhere to buy alcohol at that time…

Frantically…I searched the room…feverishly searching for what I knew would take the fear away…the pain away…but there was nothing…only empty bottles of Russia's finest…

I sat on the bed and felt the fear rise. I just wanted to cry…but I was too afraid of what was coming to shed any tears. The fear was building as my body began to spasm…and the tightening inside my stomach began…I was going into shock…I was going into withdrawal…

I couldn't sit still…

I was climbing the walls...my heart was racing and my panic was rising. I knew what was coming because I'd been there before...in that terrible place where most people with my illness have been...time and time again...withdrawal...

My experience of withdrawing from alcohol...without medical attention...is vast and nothing less than horrific. The fear...the physical pain becomes unbearable and there's only one solution...alcohol…

Withdrawal for someone like me is dangerous...it can kill...

Heart racing...panic attacks...convulsions...stomach-churning gagging...

Pacing the tiny room...over and over again...pacing and pacing as the withdrawal took it's grip...as my illness hurt me…

In this miserable state...I would do anything for a drink...anything to make the pain go away...make the fear subside and once again allow me to sink into that comfortable nothingness...a nothingness that an alcoholic like me knows only too well. Alcohol...my saviour and my sanity. That's how insane my reality had become...

Constantly looking at my watch to see if any time had passed...no time…

I did that for five hours...all the time my body gripped in spasms...screaming for a release from the pain...screaming for alcohol. I did that for five hours...

I staggered to my feet and somehow made it over to the broken mirror on the wall...the stained wall above the dirty sink. My face was swollen...red...skin covered in slime. My eyes were yellow...my eyes were bleeding. I was dying...

Why?

Leaning against the dirty sink...filled with dozens of cigarette butts and vomit...I stared into the mirror and asked myself...

What happened to you? Where did it all go wrong?

The same questions...over and over again...the same questions for five hours...the same baffled and confused stare at my reflection as the horror of my situation played over and over in my mind....not the situation of having lost everything in my life...the situation of having to somehow dig deep within myself...to find the strength...the will to endure the madness long enough until I could buy more alcohol. My will was powerful but my body was shutting down...

Legs buckling through exhaustion and a craving for relief...I sat once again on the edge of the bed with no covers. I looked down at my swollen   stomach...so painful...bladder filled with what was left from my vodka frenzy from hours before. I needed relief but there was no toilet in the small dark room. The bathroom was in the hallway...only yards away from where I sat...but I didn't want anyone to see me...yet at the same time all sense of decency had been abandoned for weeks as my only thought was how I could my next drink...

My stomach was swollen and the pain was adding to the stress of my withdrawal...the solution was simple to my state of mind...

I undid the buttons of my combat trousers and relieved myself over the edge of the bed and onto the carpet. The stream of hot steaming urine seemed endless as it splashed onto the floor...soaking one of my feet which was without a sock. I didn't care about the consequences or the smell. I was a human being lost in the most misunderstood illness known to the world...lost and without dignity...

Empty and lost...

The emptiness I felt during those hours...empty of any kind of feelings...surrounds me now as I write…

I know that I'm no longer there anymore...yet the feeling of numbness embraces me once again as I write these words…

There is a realisation that I'm no longer in that dark place...a darkness in my life that seems so long ago...all of seventeen months…

The feeling of nothingness had embraced my life for such a long time that I'd conditioned myself to not feeling much at all...devoid of feelings for years…

The reality is...as I know now….I could and did feel...I just didn't know how to process them for what they were...a common thread that seems to link us all together...people like me...people who live with my illness…

So it was with a feeling of emptiness that I emptied myself onto a very worn and very seventies style carpet...in a homeless hostel on the east coast of England...

My life had been reduced to this state and I felt nothing. My life had been a success and all of that success had gone...taken away by myself and my illness…

Only five years earlier...I had been enjoying lunch alongside Royalty in Edinburgh. My life was no more and everything that I had worked hard for had gone...all who I had loved wanted nothing to do with me…

It seemed my end was close...yet all I could think of was my next drink. A summer's morning was breaking outside...so I began struggling to get dressed. My clothes were ragged and stank of urine...but I didn't care...my only thought was buying alcohol...

My immediate reality was that I could barely walk…

I stumbled down the two flights of carpeted stairs that saw me find the reception area. I was so happy to find that there was no-one around to see the state that I was in...no-one to see my truth…yet it would have been   impossible for them not to know that I was chronic and in serious trouble…

The walk from the hostel to the shop was terrible. Weak with exhaustion from having not eaten in a week...my body in spasms...baulking bile…I almost passed out on the pavement…

There was no way that I could walk properly...so I stopped trying to pretend that I could...and staggered my way along the busy rush hour sidewalk towards the shop that sold what I needed...what my body craved…

Somehow...I managed to make it. I was early and had to wait for twenty minutes for the shop to open. I stood outside the premises...hunched over with fear at what I had become...nothingness…

Life walked by on their way to work. People strolling with a purpose in the early morning sunlight with thoughts of what lay ahead for them in whatever it was that they did for a living...people who had something to live for...people with lives and friends and family...the living. My life was gone and I didn't care...not for them or for myself. I actually stood and watched them walking by...watched them and pitied them as they strolled on towards their mundane existence...my insanity was almost complete…

The placebo effect of my imminent purchase embraced me with a sense of relief. Then...a question to myself…

Why does Ipswich stink of piss?

The smell of urine then walked in as the shop doors opened...

No!

I began to cry when the shop owner refused to sell me two bottles of vodka…

The woman behind the counter told me leave the premises and to see a doctor. My fear escalated to blind panic as I begged her to help me...begged her to sell me the bottles. I fumbled inside my pocket and produced the money needed to buy the alcohol...she wasn't interested…

Tears were streaming down my face as I confessed to being an alcoholic. I was expecting pity...what I found was a woman who saw my truth and my truth was that I was in trouble...my truth was that I was likely to end up dead if another drop of alcohol were to pass my lips. The woman behind the shop counter did the right thing...she could have made a profit that day...instead...she refused to serve me and told me to get medical help. The woman then told me to leave her premises or she would phone the police…

I pocketed my cash and staggered out of the shop...

My admission to being an alcoholic was dishonest. Despite my terrible circumstances...I remained in denial. I knew it had all gone horribly wrong...but I couldn't seem to marry the substance abuse with my problems...my consequences. I only confessed to being an alcoholic to find pity...to manipulate the situation so that I could get what I wanted...what I needed…

I didn't find pity that morning...I found compassion. One human being saw another in distress and the result was genuine concern from a caring place...*See a doctor!*

The woman saw the truth of me...a truth I couldn't see. Blinded by my illness...I left the shop...still in tears and with a new-found resolve...not to find medical help...to find a way to get what I needed...

I'll do anything...

When someone like me is in active addiction...I will do anything to get what I need to make the pain and the fear go away...

Once again I found myself standing outside the shop on that sunny summer's morning...and once again I stood in shock as life strolled on past me...

My cash was still in my hand. The nearest store that sold alcohol was almost a mile away...my body was shutting down and I was   losing the final pockets of strength that I had within me...so something had to be done quickly...

It was at this point in my madness...standing on the pavement...that I reached what is referred to in addiction as my *rock bottom*...

The people walking on their way to work...the same people who I had earlier pitied for their mundane existence...were to be my   salvation in getting what I needed. Wearing filthy and ripped clothing...stinking of urine, vomit and alcohol...I asked complete strangers if they would go into the shop and buy vodka for me?

When making this request to these people...it was at that point that I lost all respect for myself...all respect for them...

Three people were subjected to my pleas for help in buying what was essentially killing me...three times I was rejected with looks of anger and contempt...

Not only was I hurting myself...but I also hurt those who I asked for help. I saw the fear in their eyes as they saw my truth...a truth that scared them...

To me...that was my *rock bottom*...but it was to get worse as that summer's day continued...as I staggered on down the street in my own madness...

I found my salvation...

The memory of how I eventually found the vodka still eludes me. I must have somehow managed the mile walk into the town centre...despite my body shutting down...

Hours after the lowest point in my active addiction...I found myself back in the small stinking room of the homeless hostel...two plastic carrier bags filled with alcohol at my feet…

A bottle had already been opened and half of the contents were gone. I had found a shop somewhere...bought the vodka...walked outside onto the street...opened the bottle...swallowed half...in front of anyone who happened to be walking by…

What people thought of me was no longer an issue...I had reached new depths...touching the bottom…

It would have been highly unlikely that I would have made it back to my room if I hadn't managed to get strong alcohol into my body...the withdrawals would have eventually brought me to my knees…then into an ambulance...another ambulance...so many over the years...

So I made it back with bags filled with alcohol….this time no joy at my success...another realisation was replacing the usual elation. Sitting on the edge of my bed...covered in week-old sweat and stink...I opened up the   bottle again and began drinking myself into another state of unconsciousness…nothingness...

The sounds of that summer's day breezed their way through my open window as the warm and welcome glow of the vodka filled me from within...a beautiful and welcome relief...relief to body and mind empty of the spirit it so desperately needed to feel...

Drifting into the blackness...the solution appeared before me...and for the first time in so many years...I felt at peace...

It was the afternoon when I awoke...

Once again the realisation of where I was and what was happening...once again filled with fear...

My first thought was alcohol...nothing less...

Terror gripped me as I couldn't remember if there was anything left over from my earlier binge...

Oh God please...please God please...

I slumped over the edge of the bed and looked down onto the floor...two full bottles of vodka were in full view...my relief was overwhelming...

Time and time again I had awakened from the blackness...only to find that all of the bottles were empty. An alcoholic can go into a state of *blackout*...awaken and continue to drink...pass out again...and never remember...

Despite my state of mind...despite my distress at what had become of me...I still remembered the choice I'd made before drinking   myself into a state of unconsciousness...only hours earlier...

My decision bestowed me with a sense of calm as I opened one of the two bottles remaining...my final two bottles of alcohol...my last ever...

The solution had been made clear to me...a solution so simple...simple in taking all the pain away...making everything right again...

It seemed to me that I'd found serenity as the realisation of what I needed to do became so obviously simple and clear...

Remove the problem and all of my problems would be removed...

I was the problem...

I gave myself thirty minutes to drink as much as I could...smoke a few cigarettes...then get rid of the problem...

The problem was me…

The problem was me and I was hurting those who loved and cared for me…

My hurt to them had gone on for long enough and now it was time for the hurt to end...my end…

I loved them all so much and I knew that they would miss me terribly...mourn me and suffer in a terrible way in knowing that they would never see me again…

Those who loved me...those who cared for me...they would miss me...but in time...they would forget me and their hurt would subside as they moved on with their lives...on their own journeys in this life…

My end would hurt them...but it was so clear to me that I had to meet my own end so that they could be spared...spared the fear and hurt at seeing me this way...spared in seeing what I'd become…

My failure in life had to end...for the sake of those who loved me…

I believed that once gone to wherever I was going...once it was done...I would ask if I could return to watch over them and be with them...make sure that no further harm would come of them…

Belief is something that I've always had...even in that stinking room...and it was with this faith that I made a decision to end myself...so that I could care for those who loved me...care for them and stop their pain…

The way out had become clear...a moment of clarity in the darkness of where I was...the way out had become clear and the way out was through the window of the room for the homeless…

I calmly sat and drank...I calmly sat and smoked...I even listened to some music...watching the seconds tick by as time approached my deadline...

It went quickly…

For days…time had passed so slowly as I sat in my alcohol-fuelled mire…

Now…it was time…

Staggering to my feet…I took one final look into the broken mirror and stared straight at what I saw…nothingness…

I grabbed the chair and pushed it up against the wall…below the open window…

Pulling myself up and onto the chair…I leaned out…then down…and saw the pavement so far below…

There were three people standing below…just standing and talking to one another…an older man and two young women. The trio stood below…to the left of where my fall would take me…so I was grateful for that…grateful that they wouldn't be hurt…

My thoughts during those final seconds are clear. At the very least…multiple injuries…body broken…these injuries would stop the pain. Ideally…if I could land on my neck…the outcome should be final…

The drop was at least thirty feet…one final fall…one final fall to grace…grace from which I had fallen…one final fall would stop my hurt to others…

I leaned back into the room…on top of the chair…just enough distance to be able to throw myself forward….

There was just enough strength left within me…with the little that I had left within me…I grabbed the sides of the window…and with force…threw myself forward…

This was no cry for help…no plea for another chance at life…

I threw myself with such force at the open window…

It was the top floor...window left…

Struggling...fighting…

I couldn't make it through the opening...

I found myself stuck…

Hanging high above the pavement...my body was jammed at the waist in the metal frame…

The man and the two women were still standing on the pavement below... oblivious to what was going on so far above them. All I could think was…

Please don't look up...please don't see me like this...

My image…

Despite the horror of what was going on for me…despite what I was doing to myself…my only thought was what others would think of me…suspended high above and with the sole intention of ending my own life…

It was insane…I was insane…

Then my sanity abandoned me altogether…

In that moment…a realisation…a moment of clarity about something that had always bothered me…something I'd never really been able to understand…and it took that desperate moment in my life to become enlightened to what it meant…

So this is what they mean when they say…is the glass half full…or half empty?

Despite what was happening…my darker-than-dark sense of humour remained…a welcoming comfort for me as my sanity had clearly jumped out of the window before me…

I began to laugh to myself…

Somehow…I managed to wriggle myself free and ended up back in the room where I sat on the edge of the bed…

The laughter departed…hopelessness returned and once again I found myself in the grip of my own darkness…nothingness…

I felt lost as my only hope had gone…lost as I realised that I couldn't even end my suffering and the suffering of those I loved. The sense of uselessness amid the nothingness overwhelmed me…I couldn't even end my own life…useless…

Sitting alone in the stinking room…I felt the tears well up from deep within me…then…my phone rang…

The ringing broke my isolation...

For one full week...I had sat alone...drinking...willing no contact with the world around me...

My phone was ringing and something inside me sensed to me to answer the call...so I did...

His name is Ed and he was my community psychiatric nurse...a kind and caring man...a gifted professional in his field of mental health care...a man who had done everything to help me get well...to help me heal from the harm that I was doing to myself...

Ed had spent eight long months doing his best to treat me and to help me to find peace with myself...and time and time again...it had always ended in a dark place...my dark place...and by my own doing...

He asked me where I was. I answered. He told me to stay put as he would be with me within twenty minutes. I said I would remain in the room. He told me there was one final option...there was one final chance for me...

I promised Ed that I wouldn't move until he arrived. A chance...I had a chance...

I sat on the edge of the bed and became aware of a sense...a feeling that I'd forgotten...something that I hadn't felt for such a long time...Hope...

Looking down at the worn seventies carpet...I saw that there was still some vodka in one of the bottles. I didn't pick it up...

I'm sitting in tears as I write these words.. Hope...

There was no urge to drink before he arrived. I just sat and waited. My friend Ed arrived in the stinking room with two precious gifts. The first was himself...the second was the beginning of my recovery from alcohol...

Chapter Three

One Final Chance...

Slow and painful...

Ed took me to the place I'd been so many times before. St Clement's Psychiatric Hospital in Ipswich...

This place of healing for the mentally unwell had become a familiar setting for my detoxing...too familiar...especially for the staff who were doing the best that they could to see me well...

My illness is the most misunderstood. The medical profession has little insight into what is needed to save a life...a life like mine... from an illness like my illness. That's my own personal view...

Admission for yet another detox found me with a sense of dismissal from the staff...professionals in the industry of care who must have been exasperated...weary of once again admitting this hopeless alcoholic...me...who relapsed time and time again...

I have the greatest respect for the staff at St Clement's...for the medical profession...they did their best for me over and over again...but the solution to find hope for the hopeless can only be found elsewhere...

My physical detox began...my spiritual detox would take place elsewhere...

Librium...lots of Librium was needed. The medication calms the anxiety...the fear and stress...that withdrawal from alcohol induces. It was the final detox that I've ever had to suffer...it was the most horrific. Even with the medication...I found myself in my own waking terror...

The fear I felt is indescribable...not only the stress to my body...but also the stress of knowing I'd lost everyone and everything...

I'd almost lost myself to the world. A man lost to himself. A man lost to life...

I was a man lost to people, places and things...

I used to be someone in the world...or so I thought…

All was lost as I sat alone in the secure psychiatric unit...

Loved ones...friends...home...career...all was gone...hope was gone…

Sitting in my room...I listened to the sounds of what was happening within the unit...sometimes quietness...sometimes screaming. The realisation of my place in life left me so fearful that I could barely breathe. The terror of awakening to the insanity of where I was...again...the insanity of what I had become...the terror tightened around me...

Hope was lost and I sat hopeless on the edge of my bed. I didn't want to leave my room for fear of what people thought of me…

Time and time again the staff had helped me to detox...time and time again I would relapse following discharge...time and time again I was taken back to the secure unit...I couldn't face them…

I've lost count of the number of detoxes that I've been admitted to since 2006. It must be around twelve or thirteen...each one two or three weeks at a time...6 months of my life spent in the grip of the horror of an alcohol detox. Six months of my life…

Fearful of walking out of my room and into the ward...I lay down on my bed ...overwhelmed by fear...overwhelmed by guilt...overwhelmed by shame...overwhelmed by a sense of nothingness for me and my life…

The tears filled my bleeding and yellow eyes...then streamed down my sore and swollen face...drops of fear from deep within me…

The fear and pain at knowing what was coming...the fear and pain of knowing what the night was to bring...the fear of knowing it was always worse in the darkness of night…

The night of time...

She comes to me in night time

And to see me as I sleep,

She comes to me in night time

And to see me hurt so deep,

She comes to me in night time

Under inky blackened sky,

She comes to me in night time

So to hold me as I cry...

She holds me close in night time

As in fear I face my fate,

She holds me close in night time

As I wish on Heaven's Gate,

She whispers close in night time

Words of hope from high above,

She whispers in the night time

Of for me celestial love...

And when upon the night time

Want of hurt her heart does break,

So then upon the night time

Smiling grace upon my sake,

And so into the night of time

She holds my soul so near,

With light into the night of time

She blesses every tear...

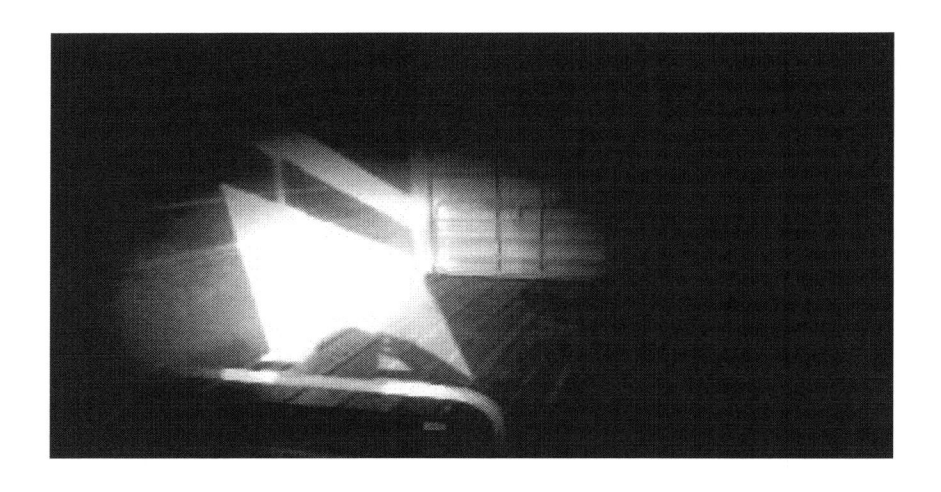

The bed...the room...fear...

Facing fear was nothing new to me…

Growing up during the Apartheid regime...fear had presented itself to me in its ugliest form...man's ill-will to fellow man at its worst. But nothing could ever prepare me for a first night of detox...nothing…

In bed...alone and in the darkness...my body and my soul screamed out for relief from the craving for alcohol. Even with the high dose of medication to help me relax...I was terrified…

Sleep was impossible…

In and out of bed...pacing the dayroom of the ward...sitting and walking and walking and sitting. Pleading with the nursing staff to give me something...anything to help me to relax...anything…

There was no more and I would have to wait until morning for the next dose...they were only doing their job. I had to somehow dig deep and get through the night...through the darkness and into the light of day…

I prayed for the morning to come...

Sitting alone in the semi-darkness of the dayroom…

Distraught…panicking…seconds would pass and I would once again pace the room…the hands on the clock were motionless…no time was passing and the fear within me was building…

Time and time again I tried to find solace in having a cigarette. Time and time again I would find myself inhaling…then vomiting nothing from deep inside of me. Dehydration…no sooner did I drink water…no sooner it came back up again…

My body wanted and needed one thing and one thing only…but that was never going to happen…I was locked in…

I walked the corridors of the unit…walked and walked and walked…then into a bathroom to try and find some relief for my swollen stomach…so swollen…

Unbuttoning my trousers…I sat on the toilet…begging for relief. Nothing happened…nothing came out. I lifted my shirt and looked down at my stomach…round and hard…covered in a red rash. Then I noticed my   manhood…it was barely there…pulled into me and barely visible. My body had decided that my bowels weren't needed to keep me alive…so those parts had been shut down…

Pulling myself to my feet…I staggered over to the sink to wash my face. The mirror welcomed me with something else that was disappearing…my humanity…

The reflection brought me face-to-face with my illness…matted hair…yellow bleeding eyes…face swollen…skin red and peeling. Staring into my aching eyes…I thought I saw a glimmer of something I'd never seen before. My spark of life from deep within me seemed to be fading away…

John was nearly gone...

It went on and on...it went on for hours...

I can't do this anymore...please...I can't do this anymore...

The words rang hollow within my own emptiness. Words I'd promised to myself in so many detox units up and down the country...always with the intention of fulfilling them...always with an attitude of arrogance once I was released from the hospital...followed shortly after by a delusion that I could control my intake...so many times...

Chronic...progressive...life-threatening illness...

There was something different about this night...a night like so many others that I'd suffered...something had changed...something so far away...so far away and deep within me...it seemed to hear my words...

Please...I can't do this anymore...please...

Pleading for a life...I made a decision to fight...I made a decision to fight for my life. It seemed there was something after all...something left within me...within the nothingness inside of me...

I staggered to my room and fell onto the bed. Curled up beneath the covers...my heart racing...racing and with every breath embraced by a heavy guttural sigh...I somehow managed to drift off into some kind of peace...some kind of peace from my reality...

Lying on my side...transfixed by what I could see before me...I watched as they entered my room...then left my room...for the remainder of the night. A man and a woman...each taking their turn to sit with me and reassure me that all would be well...smiling at me with kind eyes...smiling as they showed me a film of my life...my life that had so very nearly ended that day...

The man and the woman were showing me Hope...

Silence isn't a word I would associate with a psychiatric ward…

The sounds of minds unwell awaken the other minds unwell and so a new day begins…the lost in the world of mental health problems all together in a secure unit…

During my amassed six months in these places of healing…I would sometimes sit alone and wonder how I'd managed to end up in a place …a place where sick minds were the focus of care…

My illness wouldn't allow me to admit that I was insane…sanity had long since departed and the madness of repeated relapse and suicide attempts shone the spotlight on my state of mind…

Attitude and behaviour…active addiction…despite my terrible track record… I would be discharged from every hospital feeling better…confident…egotistical and arrogant…easily convincing myself that I could control my drinking…

Hospital detoxes were dangerous for me. They fixed my body over a short period of time…but my illness is in my mind…my illness is an addictive personality…fuelled by fear…

Alcohol is simply a symptom of my disease…my illness is me…

My attitude in thinking I could control everything…including drinking…that attitude is life-threatening as my behaviours have shown…

I awoke amid the early morning sounds of sick minds crying out for help…sounds that had by now become a comfort to my own state of mind…only because I'd heard them all so many times before.
Awakening to the new day…I remembered the man and the woman…the man and the woman who had been with me during the small amount of time that I'd somehow managed to find solace in sleep…

A man and a woman…

They were in my thoughts as I emerged from my room…

I was also aware that I needed to find the strength to somehow take a bath…I knew that I looked awful…I knew I smelled even worse…

The memory of the man and the woman…the couple who took turns in sitting with me only hours before…was still so vivid in my mind…I needed to find out who they were so that I could thank them…

Washing was difficult but delivered a sense of relief in feeling clean…and that made me feel a bit better…

My anxiety had relaxed a little…but still very much lost in a dark place within myself…

Tea and coffee was available in the dayroom and I did my best to get something into my stomach. I managed a small amount and that in turn handed me another small relief…small steps…

Sitting alone on one of the sofas…I watched as other patients struggled with their own minds…

Please…I don't want to be in a place like this again…please…

One of the nurses was sitting nearby…so I asked her about the man and the woman…the people who had helped me…reassured me…in my room during the night?

My request was met with a look of puzzlement…a look of concern…

I smiled a *thank you* and looked away…away and out towards the window from where another beautiful summer's day was dawning…dawning for those locked within the place of healing…

So no-one had entered my room…no man…no woman. A sense within me told me otherwise…a sense that was to awaken as the events of the weeks and months that were to come …

A sense…

A sense of surrender was also within me…

The profession of care...care for the lost...had one final option for me...residential rehabilitation…

Several days had passed since my admission to the ward and it was at this time that I met her...the wonderful woman who would see me sent away...sent away to a place of hope...the *Place of Miracles*...

Cynthia is a kind and caring woman...a woman with great insight into helping those who suffer in addiction...the woman who made all of the necessary arrangements for me to begin my recovery in a far away place…

We met in a small room within the unit...and when she met me...I felt like a broken man. The fight had gone...and with that...came a glimmer of hope from deep within me…

It seems...as I write this now...that it was my very beginning...my own epoch in a life of light...one single moment when my surrender began...a surrender that was to deliver so much more in the months to come…

We talked for a short while…only a short time before she asked me…

John...are you ready for a treatment centre?

I didn't need to think about my answer. I knew it couldn't go on. And anyway...I had nowhere else to go. No-one wanted anything to do with me...family...friends...everyone and everything had gone...along with my sense of self…

With a sigh of relief I said…*Yes….I'm ready…*

Cynthia smiled and held me close...close in my broken state. Alcohol had brought me to my knees….I will always be grateful to my illness for that...

Gratitude overwhelms me now…

Then…I was empty and without hope…feeling nothingness as Cynthia departed the psychiatric ward to begin the preparations for my journey to a rehabilitation centre…one final chance at life…somewhere…

Returning to my room…I sat on the edge of my bed…in fear once more…

There was so much fear. Rehabilitation meant a possible solution for me…but all I'd ever really known was me. Change was something I feared despite knowing that it gave me an opportunity…a chance…

Cynthia had told me that it would take time before my treatment would be approved…weeks…maybe longer…

The fear of change and the fear of having no-where to live until that time left me crippled with the terrible realisation of my situation…of my life…

Family and friends had abandoned hope…and me with it. Homeless hostels had been abused by me and there were no other options available once my two week detox was complete. I feared the worse…I feared the streets…

Despite all of this…a week after my admission…I was allowed to take a walk to the local shops on my own…a gesture of trust. I was fully aware that the staff could breathalyse me upon my return if they suspected that I'd taken alcohol…and to fail would mean immediate discharge and onto the streets…my new greatest fear…

I walked to the local store…bought a packet of cigarettes…a chocolate bar to cover the smell…the smell of the bottle of alcoholic lemonade that I'd also purchased…

My illness is powerful…

They didn't breathalyse me...

I went to my room...lay on the bed...in fear that someone would come...that someone would find out what I had done...

No-one came...

The 12th of June 2010 was the day I took my last drink...

It wasn't even enjoyable...it was just something that I did...had to do....

My name is John and I'm an alcoholic in recovery...something I now say with pride as I sit and write these words...

Without the blessing of my illness...I would never have been able to awaken to just how blessed I truly am...so grateful that I went through what I had to go through to get to where I am...where I am at this point in my life...

My blessing comes in many forms...my blessing begins with my parents...

They had to distance themselves from me...for me to find my knees...

Time and time again I begged them to allow me to live with them after I'd lost everything...time and time again they had refused...

This time something happened...it left me confused...this time they agreed for me to stay with them until I could be admitted into a treatment centre...

I'm so grateful to them for giving me that chance...gratitude now...relief then. Two weeks passed and my detox was complete. My father picked me up from the secure psychiatric ward and I bid farewell to fellow patients and to the staff. I'm quietly confident that it has a half-hearted goodbye on their part...with expectations of seeing me again. They never did...

Felixstowe...the east coast of England...

My stay with my parents was conditional...if they even suspected that I had taken anything...anything...then I would be out on the streets...

The first two weeks were a nightmare for me...constant cravings for alcohol...the emptiness within me growing...

Everything I write is honest and so the truth is this...during the first fortnight with my mother and father...if I could have taken alcohol without them knowing...I would have...

But I was watched closely...they never let me out of their sight...almost...

There were several occasions...during my stay...when I would manage to sneak away from them while out shopping. Not alcohol...but painkillers...anything to change the way I felt...anything...

Despite the warnings...the illness within me reigned supreme...consequences of my actions would have been severe...

Anything to change the way I felt was what I needed...and so I took risks...the feelings of emptiness within me demanded something...and I was powerless as my actions proved...

Although I was taking painkillers...I was resigned to going to a treatment centre. It was an acceptance that I embraced...simply because I had nowhere else to go...but I did sense a small glimmer of hope at what I would experience there...

I know what that was now...I was sensing what awaited. I was sensing who was waiting. My mother and father were anxious that I would refuse at the eleventh hour...but I knew I would go...

The sense told me so..the sense of Her...

Twelve weeks were to pass before my rehabilitation was to begin. Those three months I spent with my mother and father in their home on the east coast of England. During those three months...not one single drop of alcohol passed my lips...not one. That was a miracle in itself...

My admission date for the treatment centre was 21 August 2010...sunny with blue skies...a beautiful morning in the late of summer...

Ed arrived...my friend arrived...

It was an emotional farewell as I bid my parents goodbye...not really knowing when I would see them again…

There was no worry...there was a sense of something...a spark of strength from within me that embraced me with a feeling of hope...

Myself and Ed climbed into the car and our journey to the west coast of England began...a new journey for me as I headed into the unknown...not knowing what awaited me…

My new path had begun...

I knew I had a problem with alcohol...yet in denial of being an alcoholic…

I knew I was embarking on my final chance at life...a chance with hope. I thought I knew a lot of things...but what I didn't know...had never known...was that I was blessed with the *gift of second sight*...a blessing that would soon awaken once I'd passed through the doors of the treatment centre to which I was heading...

We drove away as my mum and dad waved goodbye. I waved back at them...unknown to me that I was only months away from being shown the truth of the greatest secret known to Humankind. I thought I knew a lot of things...I had no idea...

Do you think I'm a sociopath?

These were the words I asked of Ed as we headed west…

I asked this of him because I genuinely believed that I couldn't feel anything…anything at all…

The sense of nothingness within me had prevailed for so long that I truly believed there was something seriously wrong with me…something cold and empty that surged forth from deep within me…inhuman and cold…a sense that no other people seemed to have…

My problem with alcohol wasn't as clear to me…despite everything that had happened…the consequences of my drinking. It was the sense of not being able to feel that seemed very real and it was this sense of emptiness that I truly believed was the source of my problem…

In my mind…there was no doubt that compassion had left me…that empathy for human feeling had gone…

Ed looked across at me and with a gentle smile said…

No John. You're not a sociopath…you're ill and now you're going to a place that can help you to get better…

Ed is such a kind and caring man…as well as being a gifted professional in the field of mental health care…

I know that he almost gave up on me…he told me so. My final relapse saw me so close to seeing an ending between myself and Ed…but he made one final push for me…a last resort that saw him drive me to a place of healing on the west coast of England…

To many…this treatment centre is affectionately known as…

The Place of Miracles…

Chapter Four

Where Angels Dwell...

Broadway Lodge…

The Place of Miracles sits high above the seaside town of
Weston-Super-Mare…

Grand and gently imposing…steadfast and strong in its approach to
providing a solution to the problem…my problem…

Once an eighteenth century hunting lodge…then convent with
chapel…the Lodge has been treating addiction since 1974…

They say that Broadway is the second best rehabilitation centre in the
United Kingdom…I beg to differ…

For me…without bias…I can honestly say that it is the best in the
country…the best in Europe…the best in the world…

The Lodge is a place of healing for the lost and alone who suffer in
addiction…the miserable and the fearful. It's compassionate and fearless
in its approach in handing the solution to those who walk through the
heavy wooden doors upon arrival…

Holding those who stumble…embracing those who crawl…

The ethos is a simple...

You're here to get well...so get with the programme. It works if you work it...so work it and let the healing begin. If not...then it's your choice to return to the madness and do it all over again...all again...with the very real prospect of never making it back...

It's your choice...

I made my choice...I chose to live...

The beautiful old mansion is the keystone in healing...

It's the centrepiece in the treatment of addiction and resides amid two acres of grounds...where well manicured gardens provide a sanctuary for healing...holding those who've suffered...lost to life and lost to self...

Two hundred years of stone and mortar...four decades of delivering the solution to those willing to surrender to their illness...it carries the message of hope to the hopeless...a chance at life...

Broadway Lodge is formidable in its gentle purpose of healing...

My own hope was almost gone...

We drove up the winding driveway that welcomes every new arrival to the possibility of something special. There's a saying in recovery...*A life beyond your wildest dreams...*

My own dream of a life had become a nightmare. That was all about to change as I stepped out of the car and into the care of a place so very special...the place of Angels...

Chapter Five

The Journey Begins...

Smiling and warm…

The faces of the people who were soon to be my new friends in early recovery...my new friends in life…

They stood outside the main entrance...enjoying a cigarette break in the afternoon glow of the summer sun...warmth amid the icy grip of an illness that's so misunderstood...an illness that kills…

With smiles and handshakes...hugs and *hellos*...I was immediately welcomed into the fray…

There was a sense of something that caught me off-guard...a sense of something that I knew...but couldn't remember. It didn't take me long to figure it out...my new friends-to-be were laughing amongst themselves...they were happy…

It had been so long since I'd felt anything like that...a sense of being happy and a sense of belonging...all within a matter of minutes…

It was uplifting for me...

I excused myself and entered the old mansion building through the heavy wooden doors. Ed was with me. I was signed in and we made our way to the administration offices where my admission process would begin…

We sat together until the staff were ready for me...then it was time to say goodbye...

Giving each other a big hug...he wished me good luck...along with that magical smile...a smile that does his soul justice…

We bid each other farewell...then he was gone…

It was only then that I felt truly alone. I sat and readied myself for the beginning of my rehabilitation...and I made a decision right there and then…*I will do everything they ask of me...*

The mask…

A smile…yes…but false…

It's always the eyes that reveal the truth of within…

My out of focus admission photo says it all…a human being lost to focus of being. In denial and with a smile…emptiness and fear shining hollow from deep within and out through the eyes…it's always the eyes…

I saw so many pictures like mine during my time at Broadway. Upon completion of our treatment…we were handed these photographs to look upon…to reflect. My memories of what happened to me during those five months…these memories I will keep simple in the pages that follow…as I wrote at the beginning of my story. The real identities of others will remain confidential…I will share only my experiences and how they helped me to see the truth of my illness…the truth of me…

I'll keep it simple…it was at *The Place of Miracles* where I found honesty…where the truth blessed me with a new vision…a gift to help those who are lost to the world…

New faces surrounded me…

One by one I was to become acquainted with my new friends...fellow addicts...my peers who numbered around twenty four...

My plan was very clear to me on that first day...I would do anything to find the solution...the answer to getting everything back that I'd lost during those dark years in my own madness…

I wanted to find a way to win everything back...that was my plan…

Funding had been granted to me for Primary Care...two months of rehabilitation at the Lodge…

My plan had been thought through...four weeks would be enough...enough time to find the secret that would fix me...cure me of my problem...allow me to retain my rightful place in the world...once again…

I was deluded...I had no idea that my plan was twisted in its conception...inspired by a battered thought process conditioned by my illness…conditioned by me...

I glance back with compassion for myself then...at my plan...I really thought it was possible to get fixed and cured in a month...

There's a gentle smile now as I write these words...eighteen months following my admission to Broadway Lodge...I remain with the same treatment centre…although I am back in the world again...

It was never going to be four weeks...not for someone like me…

Chronic...

One month...I decided that I would do everything they asked of me so that I could find the solution…

Chronic and deluded...

The programme is tough...it has to be...

Lives are at stake and so the routine needs to be stern in its approach to healing those fresh out of active addiction...universally known within recovery as *The Madness*...

A large hand-held brass bell screams the beginning of every new day in primary care...early on every new day...so very early...

The thirty or so peers are divided into three groups...each group with its own group leader...

Early morning prayers and readings...breakfast...Tai Chi...lectures and workshops for all peers together...group sessions...lunch...one-to-one counselling with counsellor...group sessions...free time for assignment work...dinner...a film on recovery...free time for assignment work...lights out at 11pm...

The approach is holistic...wholesale non-stop...

There are also therapeutic duties which peers undertake throughout each day...ringing the brass bell...setting tables for meal times...clearing tables after meals...washing dishes...maintaining the library...cleaning floors...tidying outside areas...many tasks...lots of enthusiasm and gratitude for the opportunity to work hard for nothing...but it's all part of the process of straightening minds...minds twisted by years of active addiction...

It's a demanding routine...with the only brief respite taking place on Sunday afternoons...three hours during which family and friends may visit...

No television...radio...internet...mobile phones or music players. Music is allowed for one hour only...every Saturday evening...the lecture hall transforms itself into a dance floor...with a ping-pong table...unique...

It's radical and it needs to be...

Lots to learn…

Lots to learn and so much fun in doing so…

I've never laughed so much as I did during my two months in primary…I just loved every moment of it and had the time of my life…

Yes…it was hard work…the hours long…it was all about change…and I loved every minute of it…

New learning and laughter…new thinking and tears…lots of tears…

It was the most incredible experience of my whole life…so much so…I would love to do primary care all over again…just to see what kind of experience I would have…

Hey…what can I say…I have an addictive personality…

I'm so happy as I write these words…filled with fun as I recall those days…those long and busy days…finding my new self with my new friends…an experience that I will never forget…an experience that I will always be grateful for…grateful for the rest of my life…

Don't get me wrong…it was difficult…and my first experience of just how difficult it was going to be took place on my second day…

My first one-to-one counselling session with my counsellor…Michael…not his real name…a good man and an addict in recovery. Michael had been through the madness…had come out the other end…a new life…university…then helping those like him…like me…

Walking into his tiny office on the top floor of the old mansion…we shook hands and he invited me to sit down…

He asked me how I was feeling? I replied…

Fine thanks…

Fine!

Michael then explained his understanding of *fine*...

Fucked-up...Insecure...Neurotic...and Emotional. FINE...

I sat...looking straight at him...stunned...

Fine isn't a feeling. Let's try again...so how are you feeling?

Struggling...I was struggling to find a word...any word...just one single word to describe how I was feeling...

There was one thought...one possible response to Michael's question...but it came and went almost immediately. Somehow...for some unknown reason...it didn't feel right for me to explain that I thought I was a sociopath...devoid of feelings. It just seemed like the right thing not to do...not at that time...

He had caught me completely off-guard and I just sat in my chair in the tiny attic room...squirming. Michael sat opposite me...grinning with sheer delight at my clearly evident state of distress. I was going to see him for an hour every day...every day for my planned four weeks...

It was going to be a along squirm...

Michael could see that I was powerless over my inability to answer his question...so he didn't take pity...he simply asked me to tell him a bit about myself...

My relief was overwhelming...because *ME* I could talk about. One hour was to come and go...sixty minutes of me talking about what *ME* had done...achieved...during my life...

Michael sat silent during my enthusiastic delivery of self. When my grandiose barrage ended...it was with a smile that he said...

Good...I'll see you tomorrow...then you can tell me how you feel...

I was terrified…

Standing outside Michael's attic office…staring at a spot on the carpeted hallway…the fear was building from deep within me…

Fear is a feeling…

Michael knew exactly who and what I was…I was afraid…I was a man in fear…

All that time…all that time when I truly believed that I couldn't feel…the reality was that I'd been living in fear for most of my life…unaware…

The sad truth for me…for many…is that I'd never really talked about how I truly felt…never shared my feelings with another soul…

Society…the world…had taught me that it was a weakness to share with others my feelings…as opposed to my thoughts…so I didn't…

So the very thought of having to talk about how I felt…something that I had never shared before…shared with someone I didn't know…left me terrified…

Standing in the hallway…fearful of knowing I would have to do something that I had never done before…I would have to 'let someone in'. I felt vulnerable…I felt afraid…

It was a forty-two year old scared and lonely man who walked away from Michael's office that day…and it's one of the most powerful memories that I have of my time at Broadway…

The tears welled-up within me as I walked down the two flights of stairs to re-join my new friends…my peers…

Good. I'll see you tomorrow…then you can tell me how you feel…

Sharing my feelings was about to begin…and that meant my recovery was about to begin…

I didn't sleep well that night...

Lying in my bed in the dark...a large shared room with three other men...I just lay in dread of what the following day would bring...

Peering into the darkness...I whispered honest words to something that I couldn't see...silent words which I believed would be heard. My prayers began almost as soon as I arrived at Broadway...they continue to this day...and I'm not a religious man...

Why can't we...don't we...talk to each other with honesty about how we feel?

For me...it seems that we've lost something so important...something that can heal us...open and honest sharing about our own feelings...with other people...

The morning came after a sleepless night for me and I walked into Michael's office for my daily one-to-one...

I began to share with him...with great difficulty...what I thought or didn't think I was feeling...

It was the beginning for me...the true beginning of my recovery...

Nothing in life comes easy...the simple things can be the most difficult to embrace...

Michael sat and listened as I struggled to share my emotions...but with patience and guidance...I began to talk about how I felt...my feelings on how I saw myself...my feelings on my place in the world...

The coming days and weeks saw me open up more and more with my counsellor...my confidence grew in sharing my emotions and I gradually realised that I had nothing to fear...nothing to fear at all...

The healing had begun for me...small steps...small steps in being honest and having nothing to fear about being truthful...

Steps and Honesty...

They go hand-in-hand for me in my recovery…

The Place of Miracles works the Twelve Step Programme...the stairway to sobriety embraced by Alcoholics Anonymous…

Simply speaking...it's the Fellowship...it's The Steps...and for me it's the embrace of Honesty within The Steps that works the magic…

So I'd begun to share my feelings...I was getting honest...and for me...honesty is the secret to the healing of the Steps…

Within two weeks I started to feel better...I began to feel alive...all because I was sharing my truth…and working on Step One…

We admitted we were powerless over alcohol and that our lives had become unmanageable…

Lots of written work...the truth of my consequences during my madness…pages and pages and pages…

The truth of my illness began to awaken within me...the proof was staring me in the face...words that I'd written...lines of consequences...I WAS powerless over alcohol…

Sharing...being honest...getting vulnerable with my truth with my peers...it all began to work. I was beginning to heal. Denial of who and what I was had begun to ebb away…

My honest surrender to being an alcoholic took place around three weeks into my treatment. I don't remember the exact day...but I do remember the exact moment...one single moment in time I will never forget...

It was gentle…

It was beautiful…

It was profound...

Chapter Six

Awakening to Heaven......

Miracles do happen…

I know this because I see them all around me now. Miracles do happen and this was my first…

Step One was working on me...my honesty in facing my consequences was awakening my surrender to being an alcoholic...and more......

One sunny morning...a few weeks into my treatment...I found   myself standing in the lecture hall with my peers. All I really remember...is looking down at the parquet flooring...in my own silence amid the chatter of my friends. Staring at a single spot on the floor...I made a decision. My admission was honest...from so deep within me...and it was total…

I looked up from the floor...looked across the room...looked out through the large bay windows and out into the gardens.
Branches...leaves...bristled gently in the breeze...sunlight glimmering through the trees from the sky beyond…

Words from so very deep within me...*I can't do this anymore. My way in this world doesn't work. I'm willing to do it your way...*

Surrender…total and honest…

It was an honesty from deep inside me…a sense of my own truth from within the very essence of me…

No sooner had I silently spoken those words of surrender…the most beautiful and gentle explosion took place from deep within my chest…boom…

Then…the weight of the world just seemed to lift from me…rushing upwards and outwards…through my back…my shoulders…my head…

Elation…

I simply stood on that spot…that spot in the lecture hall…filled with joy…and it was beautiful…

You see…it was with total honesty that I admitted to being powerless. Not just over my illness…but over all…powerless over everything…

I can't do this anymore. My way in this world doesn't work. I'm willing to do it your way…

I've always believed in something far greater than me…an unseen essence around us. I've always believed…

The weight of the world lifted from within me and it was replaced with joy. I walked out of the lecture hall…laughing and joking with my peers…at peace with myself and the world…

I knew that something very important had just happened to me…but I had no idea just how important…

My spiritual awakening had begun…a light of love from the heavens was holding me close…my life would never be the same again…

It's all about the truth…

As I write these words...the rain falls gently outside my bedroom window...falling steadily from Celeste on this November night…

11.11.11…the ones...

The water falls...it cleanses...as words of truth cleanse fear...

Step One...honesty…and so all the Steps thereafter. Honesty isn't easy...fear makes it so...fear of consequences…

Once the fear of consequences is removed...removed with faith...then the truth between two human beings becomes open...no fear...therefore no anger. It's that simple for me…

Take away fear...and we take away anger and hate. Imagine...no anger and hate...our world would be a different place...the Eden it could be…

These words I write...these lines I assemble...they're written by me...inspired by the love I see all around me...the unseen…

Love in light...white light…

It's all about the truth…

The Twelve Steps are about honesty...the truth of one's self…

The Twelve Steps are about honesty and the healing that takes place when embracing the truth of one's self…

The Twelve Steps were given to those who suffer in addiction...but I've been shown that they are for the world to use...to use so that anyone can recover from themselves and from life…

Honesty. Open mindedness. Willingness. The three. All powerful...embracing the three has seen me blessed with a beautiful gift...and you can have it too...

My awakening of spirit…

Joyous for the rest of the day...laughing and joking with my peers...inspired...a sense of what it really feels like to be alive…

My elation lasted for three days…

The morning following my lecture hall experience...I found myself eating a yogurt for breakfast...along with my friends in the dining hall…

Then...out of nowhere...a song just appeared in my head...

There were no words...only music...and I'd never heard it before in my life. Sitting…eating...smiling...I listened. Then...it dawned on me that I was experiencing something profound…

Excusing myself from the table...I went to the quiet boardroom where I sat and wrote some lyrics…

Later that day...I entered Michael's office...then sitting down...I asked him if it was okay to sing? He looked a bit startled to be honest. I broke into song and delivered an enthusiastic rendition of my heavenly tune. Once the final middle-eight was done...Michael sat and just looked at me for a few seconds...slightly baffled and very confused. The he said...

That was nice…

Michael's tone of voice delivered a sense of no appreciation for my Grammy nominee...a sense which I resented...

You see...my awakening had opened a spiritual door...joyous...but there was still much work to be done. My arrogance and ego were still very much at large...and who better that my counsellor to take some spirited action. I needed to find humility…

I feel humbled as I write these words…

Humility and gratitude…they awaken a purpose within me…all powerful they are as I write these words for you…

My initial plan of four weeks passed and so I made a decision…two months in primary care wasn't going to be enough…let alone one month…I needed to go the distance at *The Place of Miracles…*

My choice to continue with treatment was based on the reality of my illness. Alcoholism is all-powerful…cunning…insidious…I needed to learn as much as I could about myself to stand a chance in the world…

Halfway through primary…I applied for funding for secondary treatment…a further three months of rehabilitation at Broadway…

I will do everything that they ask of me…

The decision to stay longer belonged to me…I know now that I was also being guided to do so…guided by the light so white around me…

My will to stay was also influenced by the Lodge and what I was learning within the mansion walls. The rigorous routine…growing relationships with my peers…gaining valuable insight from staff…I found it all inspiring…

This new lease of me was evolving…thanks in part to the incessant group sessions that we undertook on a daily basis. Peers challenging fellow peers to get to the truth…the truth of each other. Once there…we faced our fears together…growing together and learning that fear can be faced with honesty…and a belief that something greater than ourselves was with us…watching over us…

The word God plays an important part in the Fellowship…a *God of my understanding*…or *Higher Power*…

Honesty is the foundation of my recovery…honesty sees my faith…

We found our faiths together...

We found our faiths together and we found our faiths in love...

Sharing with one another on how we saw our higher powers...it all came down to love...

Love of something or someone...it was and is love that replaces the emptiness within...once an person truly surrenders to being powerless over an addiction...

The obsession to drink or take drugs can be removed...with love taking its place in many shapes and forms...

Faith in something far more powerful is different for all of us...

For some of my peers it was their children...faith in the young lives they were blessed with. For others...a parent lost to life...or a sunrise...or even the fellowship itself...higher powers come in all shapes and sizes...

They come in many forms...and they all embrace love...

My early days saw me embrace my creativity as my higher power...my love of words. My spiritual awakening had indeed opened another door within me...heightening my senses even more...senses that I'd always been aware of but never explored...through fear...fear of the unknown...

Fear knocked...faith answered...and there was nothing there...

The ability to sense fear in a room has always been with me. I sensed that my awakening was to be used to help others...those in fear...

found our faiths together and strong bonds of trust were developed. Powerful relationships were forged through finding our truths with one another...removing the fear of being honest with each other...

The truth heals...but for the truth to heal...the hurt has to be shared...

Sharing heals…

When people share their thoughts and feelings openly within one another…it removes fear…

Sharing heals and also serves another very important purpose in recovery. When one person shares…others can identify…

Those in the madness of active addiction feel that they are the only ones suffering…suffering alone and unwanted…

Sharing in the treatment centre showed me that I'm not alone in how I feel as a human being…it also showed me I was never alone in what I experienced during my time in the madness…our consequences are all very much the same…

Sharing experience…strength…and hope. The essence of every AA meeting around the world…

My first-ever share took place only four weeks into my treatment. Someone from AA was supposed to share for us one glorious September evening. The lecture hall had been set up…chairs arranged in the usual circle…peers outside enjoying the beautiful weather…as well as a cigarette…

Then…the news…no share…there had been a mix up with the booking…

Something within me told me to do the share myself. The thought scared me at first…then I felt at peace…inspired. I walked into the mansion and asked the staff if I could do the main share?

Yes you can...

The brass bell rang. The lecture hall…the room of my awakening. We all sat together in the large circle…a ring of trust…and I began to share with my peers about my life…

Chapter Seven

The Terms of Life...

A quiet boy, a sense of soul,

You promised love, to make me whole,

A feelings boy, so much inside,

You promiser of strength and mind.

You took my hand, your words your way,

The speak made sense, I begged you stay,

Sound mind I saw, the message said,

Your sense seemed real, your path I'd tread.

That choice I walked, I felt the cries,

Your promises, became your lies,

So just a child, a special soul,

My little heart, your twisted goal.

Into the dark, your way of old,

I begged your help, no answer cold,

Still just a child, so special kind,

Alone and lost, you took my mind.

On hands and knees, in filth of mine,

I cry for love, the light divine,

She takes my hand, her truth I see,

No more alone, now held by we.

Discerning once, now seen unsound,

So twisted clear, perverse you're found,

You want my soul, no more the chase,

It's promised now to Heaven's Grace...

The Discerning Pervert, 2011

Words written to my illness

I was born in Glasgow on the 16th of December 1967…

My parents were also born in Scotland. My father...Jack...is of Scottish and Norwegian descent. My mother...Evelyn...Scottish…

I have a brother who is two years younger than me...Grant...and a sister who is two years younger than my brother...Kerry. So I'm the eldest child…

We lived in Clydebank...a town once famous for its great shipbuilding industry on the River Clyde...and where my father served his apprenticeship as a fitter and turner…

All I can remember from those beginnings in my life were of being well loved...the warmth of being inside...sheltered from the outside and the cold...surrounded by close family...grannies and aunties...uncles and cousins. Lots of relatives and lots of love...

The strike actions of the seventies led my parents to make a decision...emigration for the sake of their children and themselves. My father received two job offers from companies abroad…

The choice was Canada or South Africa…a decision was made based on my father's favorite film...so thanks to Michael Cane and *Zulu*...my family headed to the southern hemisphere...

We arrived in South Africa in October 1976…

Hot...dry...unfriendly...I felt afraid...these are my earliest memories of that country. I felt fearful from the moment I arrived...fearful and out of place. I remained fearful when I departed eighteen years   later. My sense of not belonging there never changed...and so it was with a sense of not belonging that I grew up in southern Africa...but my sense of being different didn't just apply to the country...it was a feeling of being different to everyone around me. I even feel different when I'm with my family...

Different in a land of differences...

One of my earliest memories of South Africa...

We were walking into the nearby town centre to do some shopping. We'd only been in the country for a short while and so everything was so new to me...so new to all of us...

As we walked...I remember looking at all the differences...so many things different from my home in Scotland...

The roads were wider...the cars looked strange...it was hot and dusty...the shops looked more like stalls as opposed to the shops in Glasgow...and the sea of faces...faces so different to my face...

Black people...so many black people...

I don't remember feeling scared...I just looked at all of the black faces...faces that were looking at me...

I do remember their eyes...big and brown and white...and afraid...

We walked along the pavement and passed face after face as they looked at us from shop doorways . Then...as we walked...I looked up and saw an elderly black man and black woman heading towards us. They looked up and saw us approach...lowered their eyes...and stepped off of the pavement so that we could pass them by...

It makes me feel really sad when I think about that now...the look of fear in their eyes when they looked at us...at me...but I didn't understand it at the time...

My parents had brought us to a country that offered good prospects...good education...a good future. All of this was true...true only for those with a particular skin colour...whites only...

Apartheid...

I've always felt different…

My mother says I was forthright as a child. I don't remember being like that at all…quiet…thoughtful…that's how I remember being me when so young…

Those early days in South Africa are memories that I would prefer to forget…

We moved house a lot and so that meant moving schools…disruptive years for me and I'm sure for the rest of my family too…yet I always seemed to be able to fit in wherever I went and with whoever I met…

There were many immigrant families in the various suburbs where we lived…lots of other children who hailed from all parts of the United Kingdom…families seeking a new and prosperous life far away from the industrial discontent that was taking place in our homeland. I seemed to make friends with other children quite easily despite feeling different and alone…

My primary schooling saw me met with praise for being diligent and hard-working. I was just me being me…I simply kept my head down and got on with all of the work that was expected of me…what I needed to do in order to achieve good enough grades. One day…when I was around nine or ten years old…my teacher visited my home after school just to tell my mother that she had never met such an intelligent child. That was the purpose of her visit…

Highly intelligent…perhaps. Lazy…perhaps. I seemed to live in my own little world…doing what needed to be done…

These words I write now are making me feel uncomfortable…days I would never want to endure again…days that saw me also experience the harm that alcohol causes. I was young…I was highly aware…

It must have been difficult for my parents…

My mum and dad were so young…so to relocate to another part of the world…so far away from their birthplace…with three young children…it must have presented a huge stress on their relationship…

Never during my first years in Scotland did I see my parents argue…South Africa changed all of that…

The way of life there was awash with heavy drinking…and my parents became part of that drinking culture…

Memories of being awoken in the early hours…awoken to hear them arguing following a drunken night out…my mother crying…became a regular occurrence…

I would just lie in my bed…scared…listening to the hurtful words being exchanged between both of them…

This is very difficult for me to write…these words I know they will read…but these lines I write must be the truth as I've been shown that they must be…

My parents went out quite a lot during those early days in Natal…and all I can remember was the fear I felt when they were getting ready to go out…knowing that when they returned…they might be drunk and angry with one another…

One Christmas morning…I awoke very early to find that my parents were asleep following another night out. They wouldn't awaken. I'd only known the truth about Santa for a couple of weeks…after pestering my mother for the truth. I knew where the presents were hidden…so quickly arranged them in the living area. I managed to get it all done as my younger brother and sister wandered into the room…faces filled with joy at what lay in wait for them to open. I was nine years old…

Adult child…

I grew up very quickly…

Adults and their conversations began to interest me…fascinate me…I would sit and listen to them talking for hours on end as the other children played outside…

More and more I became drawn into discussions which were very adult…mostly fear based…death…

This seemed to be a topic that arose time and time again…

For me…mankind's greatest fear…fear of the unknown…

Talked about and talked about…discussed so many times…over and over again…they talked about fear…they talked about life…

It was mesmerizing for me…the seeds of my search to find the answer to my question were being sown…sown by grown-ups talking about fear and man's ill-will to fellow man…

Should I have been allowed to listen? Probably not. But it was part of my journey in life…a very important part as it made me think about why we hurt each other…

These conversations…almost always involving alcohol…did hurt me. One time…I offered my own view on why the Holocaust happened. I was eleven years old. My parents were fighting and having a drunken argument on the causes…so to try and keep the peace…I told them it was far more complicated than what they were saying…

I was angrily told to be quiet…

From that point on…I kept my views to myself and lived in fear of expressing my opinions…low self-esteem…low self-worth…

I became an observer…

That's all it took…

It doesn't take much to damage one so young…

I've heard similar experiences from my peers…so much hurt caused by words…words filled with fear…

There are no resentments between me and my parents…I harbour no resentments against them for their behaviour in those days…just as they now hold no resentments against me for my behaviours during my active addiction…

They did the best that they could under the circumstances…circumstances that brought to the fore their own troubled pasts. You see…behaviour is learned…so in essence…they were treated the same way when they were children…

And so it goes on…

Perfect parenting doesn't exist…because perfection in a human being doesn't exist…that's what I believe. It was difficult for me and it was difficult for them…a severe country with three young children…and these words are honest…

Loving and caring my mum and dad have always been for me. I love them dear and I know they love me…

As difficult as those early years were…there was also a lot of fun to be had for a young boy. The way of life was an outdoor one and so a healthy lifestyle for me and my siblings…

My brother and me would be out all day during the school holidays…playing with friends and only returning home for dinner as darkness began to fall…a darkness I feared…

I dreaded the night for so long as a young boy. It was as if I became more aware of something when the quiet of twighlight came...

Three bedrooms…

The houses where we lived during those early years all had three bedrooms…

Being the eldest…I was given my own room…

It was very rare for me to be able to spend a whole night in my own bed. Time and time again I would wait for my parents to go to sleep and then…once the house was quiet…I would sneak into the room where my brother and sister slept…

I didn't know what was wrong…I just knew I was afraid…

When alone in my room…it seemed that I could feel someone else in the room with me…and it terrified me…

Please don't let me see…I don't want to see…

The words I said over and over again under the cover of covers…the words I said as I lay in the dark knowing that there was someone with me…someone I couldn't see…words I repeated for many years…

Running from my room…along the hallway…I would end up in bed with my younger brother and cuddle into him…still with the feeling of someone watching me…

This sense of being watched was with me a lot when I was younger. I remember more and more of it now…simply because I now know who they were…who it was that I was sensing…

At the time…I was just a young boy and my parents put it down to just being afraid of the dark. They never made a big deal out of it and I'm really grateful to them for that…

Grateful to them…grateful to the love that watches me…I see them now…I see them as I write these words…standing close…robes of brown…robes of red…robes of white…

Colour...

Man's ill will to fellow man...

I was too young to understand...aware only that people of a different colour were washing my clothes...maintaining our garden...cleaning my classroom. They weren't allowed to drink from the same water tap that I drank from...travel on the same bus...the list was long...

There were only white children at my school...

Apartheid...

Several years were to pass and then I reached my final year in primary education...I was twelve years old...

My father received a job offer in a country north of the border...a country that had only just received its internationally recognised independence...Zimbabwe...

My family headed north of the Limpopo River in early 1980...

I have so many fond memories of those days in the land of the Matabele. A beautiful country where there seemed to be a lot of smiling faces...smiling faces with different skin colours in my classroom...very different to the south...

We all seemed to get on so well with one another...boys and girls on the verge of young adulthood...and it was during this time that I gained a passion for sport...football...cricket...hockey...swimming...

Children of all colours...playing together and competing amongst one another...not only in sport...but in the classroom too. Healthy and encouraged competition between young people of all races...black...white... Asian...great days near the Equator under the African sun...

Memories so fond...memories of my parents smiling too...

It's a stunning part of the world...

The countryside echoes what Africa is...beautiful...

We spent weekends away from our home in Bulawayo...weekends with family friends who owned farms...hundreds and hundreds of acres of farmland in the African bush...

Sunny days spent barbecuing and swimming...adults drinking and laughing and putting the world to rights...

The farm was also where my brother and I learned to shoot. The new government had imposed a limit on the amount of ammunition that any one farm could own. In the wake of the Rhodesian Bush War...most farmers held small arsenals of weapons...with thousands upon thousands of rounds of ammunition. Rather than hand it over to the new lawmakers in   Harare...my father's friend would drive us men out into the middle of nowhere...where weapons were handed out for target practice to begin...hour after hour...round after round...the supply was endless...

It was all so exciting for me as my teenage years approached...no longer a child and soon to become a young man. So much awaited for me in life...as round after round exploded from the smoking   barrel of the Lee Enfield 303...smashing through the full thickness of the distant Mopani tree...my choice as a target. Blissful in showing the men that I was becoming a good shot...blissfully unaware of what it was that I was actually mastering...

Twelve years of age and so my teenage years beckoned...twelve years of age and on the brink of a new chapter in my life...a chapter that began with me drinking alcohol for the first time...

I truly believe that I was born with my illness...

Cooking sherry…

I found a bottle of cooking sherry in the pantry one day and it just felt like the right thing to do…

So I was twelve years old when I took my first drink...and it did make me feel good in as much as it made me feel different…

Remembering exactly how it made me feel is something I can't remember...but what I do recall...is that over a period of a week or so...I finished the whole bottle…two bottles to be honest...

So I kept going back for more and more...with more soon becoming empties and me waiting in fear for days...waiting for someone to notice that the sherry had disappeared...in a house where no-one drank sherry…

It was never mentioned…

That was my introduction to alcohol and I never drank again until the age of seventeen…

My primary school days were coming to an end and so with that...a new dawn for me in my young life...becoming a teenager and starting high school…

My first morning saw my mother straighten my new school tie with the words…

This is the beginning of the time that will shape you as a man. So much is going to happen to you...so much that will mould you into the man that you will become…

Leaving home that morning to begin my secondary education...her words seem almost prophetic now…

A lot was to happen...and it did shape me into what I am now...a man familiar with fear...

I hadn't done anything wrong…

Myself and all the other boys in the first year were marched from the assembly hall and across the schoolyards to where the headmaster's office was…

We weren't told why…just to walk in a straight line and not to talk…

Once outside the head's office…we were lined up against a wall and took it in turns to be beaten…

They used two offices for this purpose…a male member of staff in each room…

Standing in line…outside in the hallway with the other boys…we could hear the whipping noises coming from within the offices…and then the crying of the boys who had just been beaten…

When my turn came…I just walked in and bent over the chair…the cane struck me twice…once on the buttocks…the second landing on my lower back…

There were no tears on my part…simply because I think I was in shock…

I then left the room and found my way to my first class in secondary school…introduced myself to my new teacher…and then took great care in sitting down to open my new text book…

Why?

It was to show us what to expect if we stepped out of line…that was the reason…

Violence by one human being against another was my introduction to high school…and it was just accepted. Acceptance of this must change…the change comes in light so white…

I didn't share…

The feeling of shame stopped me from sharing what had happened with my family…so I kept it all to myself…

Needless to say…I didn't step out of line…wouldn't have stepped out of line anyway. Diligent and shy…schoolwork and the playing fields where my focus and I just got on with my early career in secondary…

High school introduced me to two passions in my life…girls and rugby…

The oval ball was alien to me and I wasn't interested. Primary school didn't entertain the sport…football and cricket were my passions then. Rugby was compulsory in secondary…my stubborn side stood fast…

Thanks…but no thanks…

Diligent and shy? Yes. Stubborn when I want to be? Oh yes…

The threat of another beating didn't even work. It took the headmaster to call my father and inform him that if his son didn't at least take part in rugby training…then the only option available…was expulsion. I opted for this option but my father disagreed…purely on the basis that there wasn't another high school in the area…and school was compulsory…

My choice was no choice…so the following day I wandered down to the playing fields with the other boys…my disdain for what I was about to have to endure clearly evident to all around. Mr Evans…a Welshman…blew his whistle and rugby practice began. Two hours later…I walked off the training field with a smile on my face…

My passion for rugby continues to this very day…

They filled me with fear…

Girls…

They filled me with fear…yet mesmerised me at the same time…

Five years were to come and go for me during that high school chapter in my life…sixty months…and every day in every week in every month…every moment I would look in awe at their beauty…

Terribly shy in the company of the opposite sex…I resorted to being the joker so that I could get close to them…

My plan of attack was a simple one…make them laugh and maybe they'll want to kiss me…

There was one problem…well…maybe not quite one…there were so many…and they were all over my face…

I truly believe that my father's Scandinavian bloodline blessed me with so many fine physical attributes…tall…blonde hair…blue eyes…broad shoulders…a sporty physique…blessed…

Unfortunately for me…my Teutonic package deal also came with acne…and lots of it…

When I realised that I could make people laugh…it seemed to mask my very serious insecurities about the way I looked…especially with girls…

The reality was that I was deeply troubled by my appearance and the terrible state of my complexion…so no self-esteem…but lots of confidence with the realisation that people liked me to perform…so I performed…and was welcomed into the throng…

In actual fact…I was one of the most popular boys in the school…but within me I felt so alone…so alone amid my assembly of schoolmates…

My popularity was short-lived...

It all came to an end in 1982...a return to South Africa beckoned due to the political instability simmering within Zimbabwe...

We'd spent two years in *God's Country*...two years filled with good times...good times which now bless me with many fond memories...

Fond memories tinged with warning signs of what was coming...

Playing cricket at school and having to stop the match because of two MiG jets going head-to-head in a high altitude dogfight directly above us...

My family and another...cowering together in the darkness as government forces clashed with opposition troops in the streets not far from where we lived...huddled together in the dark with my   father and his friend armed to the teeth with automatic weapons and hand grenades...

The warning signs were clear to see and my parents didn't have to look twice. Within a matter of months all was sold and we were returning to south of the border...South Africa once again...

Many families fled Zimbabwe this way. Many of my friends were south-bound too and very apprehensive about what awaited them...a new country...

There were no fears on my part...I was almost fully bilingual and had lived in SA before. What I didn't realise was that I'd grown in Zimbabwe...no longer a boy...I was now a young man...

Fourteen years old...I crossed the border with my family...a border guarded by armed white soldiers not much older than me. It was going to different this time...this was to be the time of real beginnings...

A time of harsh beginnings...

Racism…

The abuse of someone because of the colour of their skin is simply this…it's simply wrong…

We're all the same on the inside…the sooner this fact is embraced by all…the sooner we all have a better chance at a future where there's hope…real and honest hope…

When my family returned to South Africa in 1983…I had certain racist tendencies or views. It would be highly unlikely not to have them…simply because of where I was growing up…southern Africa…

Whatever my views were…they were about to change…and not for the better…

We settled in a suburb just outside of Johannesburg and I was straight into the local high school…

The regime was strict and discipline at the end of a stick was always at hand…but generally…there wasn't much physical abuse…well not much…

It was the abuse of the mind and how that abuse was presented…that's what was particularly insidious…

Sure…physical abuse did take place…but we were all so conditioned to being beaten for this and beaten for that…so conditioned to violence that it had lost its effect on us by midway through our high school career. It was the way in which the Apartheid ideology was presented to young and naïve minds…that was the abuse that so many suffered. Words were twisted…twisted words from a twisted regime. The pseudo-sociological and religious dogma of the day was taught in such a way that it was very much believable. Man's ill-will to fellow man abuses others through the abuse of words…

It is necessary for the indigenous races of southern Africa to be separated from non-indigenous races...so that they do not become pseudo-Europeans and lose their own ethnic identity...

There you have it...subtle and believable...

Believable to a young mind...innocent and naïve...fearful of voicing an opinion for fear of the consequences of doing so...

The justification to subjugate people who are different...is a justification based on fear...

Fear of people who look different...it all comes down to fear...

The top paragraph was in one of my history text books in high school...words I've never forgotten. The words made sense to me then...even though there was something within me that told me they were wrong...but I was too young and too afraid to disagree...to disagree would mean the scorn of the teaching staff...ridicule from classmates...

I agreed with the words and towed the party line...knowing something didn't quite sit with what I was being taught...

I've worn many masks in my life...the racist mask was once my most shameful...I say once because the unique programme that I now work has shown me that I can forgive myself...

Love and forgiveness...not synonymous with Apartheid...fear and violence on the other hand...completed the twisted trio...

Surrounded by so much fear...so much hate...so many guns...it was inevitable that I would come face-to-face with violence...

I was sixteen years old when I met the ill-will of man...within the eyes of a stranger...within the eyes of a woman...

I was sixteen years old...

That day...

Two years had passed since returning to South Africa. I was growing into a young man…a young man with twisted views of others...

Academically…I was average…though I knew I was capable of achieving so much more. On the sports field…I held my own…but it seemed that the further I moved into my teenage years…the more I seemed to lose interest in the world around me…I felt lost...

The mask was on and I was performing a role…a part in a play that I knew just wasn't for me…but from which there was no exit left of stage…

I was trapped on the right...

It was a sunny and clear winter's afternoon as I walked home from rugby practice. In a world of my own…as I've always been prone to do…I paid no attention to the black of flats as a wandered on by…

Then…a loud bang…followed by several more. The firing sounds exploded from within the ground level parking garage…underneath the block of flats that I was passing…

My immediate thought was one based on association…it must have been a car back-firing…but within seconds…the screaming began…

Standing still…I looked over to where the entrance was to the parking garage…and that was where I saw her emerge into the light...

The girl came racing towards me…screaming as she grabbed my arms and began shaking me…screaming and crying…begging me to help them. She was about my age…also in a school uniform...

Help them help them help them…

The girl's eyes were wide…terrified…and then she ran away...

Darkness…

Darkness was all I could see as I entered the parking garage from the sunny street. It took my eyes a few seconds to adjust to the blackness. The garage was small...maybe enough space for four cars...no more…

It was empty apart from a small Mazda hatchback...parked just over on the right to where I was standing. My eyes were still slightly blinded by the transition from outside...but what I could make out was that all of the car's doors were open...bags of groceries burst open and scattered on the floor…

I wandered over and looked in the boot...more bags of shopping…

Looking up and then through the rear window...I could see someone sitting in the back seat of the car...so I moved around to take a look inside…

The boy was perhaps a bit younger than me...sitting upright...his head slumped to the right and resting on his shoulder. There was a hole in the left hand side of his head...blood trickling down the side of his face. He had dark hair…he was very still...

I sensed everything around me start to slow down...time seemed to enter slow motion as I looked at the boy...slowing down even more as I gradually started to realise what I was looking at…

Slow and cold...the smell of exhaust fumes...all so very slow…

Quiet...so very quiet...as if the air had been removed from all around me...

Lifting my head out from the car...something caught my eye...over to the left and at the far end of the garage. It seemed very dark where he was...as my eyes were still trying to adjust…

It was a man...

There was no movement…

The man lay slumped on his right hand side…arms outward…still too dark to make him out clearly…

What I did see clearly…was the firearm. It lay alone in front of the still man…an automatic handgun…black…

Hesitant to move closer to the man in the dark….I just stood still and looked at him lying still…I could sense that he was also gone…

The movement…the movement just to the left of where I was standing still…standing still because I was scared of the man with the gun…the man who I knew had gone…

I looked over the where the movement had caught the corner of my eye…and that's when I saw her…that's when her eyes caught mine…

The woman was on her hands and knees…on her hands and knees and staring straight into my eyes…

Slowly…I moved back a little bit…then to my left…so that I could see her more clearly…so that I ended up standing right in front of her…looking down at where she was…from where she was looking up at me…

The woman was on her hands and knees…eyes staring into mine…mouth moving with no words. She was trying to tell me something…something for me to hear…but no words came as she mouthed her silent message to me…

Taking my eyes away from her eyes for only a moment…I looked down at the front of her body. The woman's white dress with blue flowers had fallen down to her waist…her chest exposed…exposed to me…exposed for me to see the dark shapes…three dark shapes…three black shapes from which her life was flowing onto the floor…

Life flowed from the woman…

Life was flowing from the woman who was on her hands and knees...silent words flowed from her moving lips...and life was fading from her large staring eyes...eyes staring into mine…

I couldn't move...I couldn't move and just stood and stared into her eyes…

How long we stared at each other...how long? I have no idea. It seemed such a long time...time impossible for me to measure. Bending down towards her...I looked closer into the woman's eyes...and that's when I saw life...the life of her...the essence of her spirit...disappearing from her large brown eyes…

It was at that moment that I saw something...something I'd never seen before. I saw death...only because I was seeing life ebb away from another human being...a soul drifting off…

I couldn't stop looking into her eyes...looking as I saw the very essence of her fading away...life fading away...a human life…a soul going home...

For however long we stared into each other's eyes...I believe that the woman gave me a very special gift. She showed me that life does go on...goes on to somewhere else...and with her eyes she gave me hope...hope that there is a special place...a place where we go when we pass…

I stood and watched...unable to move...and watched her slowly drift away towards that place so special…

Then...my fear lifted and I was able to think clearly...able to move. I turned and ran as fast as I could to the stairwell...running up the stairs and banging on all of the doors. Banging and thumping the doors...one eventually opened. It was an old woman...

Please call for help...

People downstairs have been shot. Please please call for help...

Frantically shouting my desperate message...the old woman ran into her flat to make the call...

I just walked away...back down the stairwell and back out onto the street where I sat on the pavement opposite the entrance to the parking garage. I sat...staring into the darkness and thinking of the woman with the eyes...the eyes that showed me so much...the eyes that showed me terror...eyes that showed me truth...

Screaming sirens...police cars...ambulances...

Many people arrived and they all ran into the darkness of the garage. I was too scared to approach them...still stunned by what had happened...so I just sat and watched all of the emergency personnel running around...

Then...after a while...the paramedics emerged from the darkness of the parking garage. The woman who had been on her hands and knees...was now lying on her back on a trolley with wheels...

As they pushed her...one of the paramedics was thumping her chest with his fist...

Halfway between the entrance to the garage...and the waiting ambulance...the paramedic stopped hitting the woman and looked up his colleagues...

She's gone...

Stunned...with a feeling of emptiness...I stood up and walked towards a plain clothes policeman. He was watching me as I approached him...and then I said...

I was here when it happened...

Life goes on…

I was interviewed by the police and then sent home…

My parents asked me if I was okay? I said…*Yes*…

Life went on for me. No counselling was offered either by the police or by my school…violence the way of life in a country torn apart by fear…

Schoolwork…sport…friends…girls…my life carried on as if nothing had happened…

Watching the woman drift from this world seemed to confirm something that I already knew…it's just that…I had no idea what it was that I knew…

That *something* I would find out many years later…

Life went on and my part in it continued. Time with my family became more chaotic…probably because there were three teenagers living in the house…my life went on…

Two options were presented to me for when I completed my schooling…university…or national service with the armed forces…

Apartheid saw young white men of age complete two years serving their country…serving an ideology that sat unwell with the outside world. Borders with Angola, Zimbabwe and Mozambique were the priority in standing guard against communism. Two ideologies at war…two ideologies clashing over words…words that denied freedom of speech…two enemies… yet allies…in denying human rights…

University or army. Choices…

My call-up papers hadn't arrived by the time I passed my final exams in 1985. My grades weren't good enough to merit university entrance. I found work with the gold mines…

The tell-tale signs…

My first experience of buying alcohol took place during my final year at school…

There was a party…we purchased our own beers…we started walking towards to venue…

It took an hour for us to walk to the party…once there…I collapsed at the gate in a drunken blackout…

We'd bought six or eight beers each. My friends still had most of their cans…my cans were empty…

The tell-tale signs of things to come for me…the signs always tell the truth…

South Africa was…and remains…an enthusiastic consumer of alcohol. Drinking is very much part of the culture…so my illness was hidden…

Those early days saw me drink a fair amount…but so did most people…so it was impossible to identify my problem…

During this time I met Jenny. It wasn't love at first sight…but our relationship was to last six years…six years during which time so much was to happen to me. Jen and me were so close at one point…so close. It's been so long since we last saw each other…I pray she's well…I pray I see her again one day…

Working on the mines…paydays…nightclubs and boozing…my way of life then…a way of life for many young men like me…

But my way of life was to change…change in a terrible way…terrible in what I suffered…yet beautiful in how I was embraced by someone…someone unseen during my suffering…

What happened had to happen. The alternative was not to be my destiny…violence was not to be my journey…

Nineteen years old…

I was nineteen years of age when I made the decision to drive to Pretoria…to volunteer to serve my country…

By now…my work with the gold mine had ended and I had landed a great opportunity with a major civil engineering company based in Johannesburg…

They were going to train me as a draftsman…I was absolutely delighted…

Only four months had passed since the beginning of my new employment…a career with prospects that involved a lot of travel around the country…

The job was great…but there was something within me…something deep inside that was looking for an answer…searching for the truth of something that had always been on my mind since that day in the parking garage…that day with the woman…the woman within whose eyes I saw the truth…

Why do we hurt each other?

That question had been on my mind for years…

Why do people do the things they do? Why do we hurt one another?

Only four months into my new apprenticeship…nineteen years of age…I made a decision to go and find the answer…

The beginning of December 1987…I jumped into my car and headed north to the capital…my destination was Army Headquarters…

To find the answer to the question that had haunted me for so long…I made a decision to go and find the answer for myself…I made the decision to wear the uniform of fear and enter the frontlines…the borders…where I believed the answers lay. I was nineteen years old…

What the fuck do you want?

He was an angry man...a small man...he was a small angry man wearing the uniform of an army commandant...

Those were the words...his greeting...as I entered his office after queuing for hours in the corridors of Army HQ in Pretoria...

Most of the young men who were waiting with me had reasons not to fight...I was different...

The commandant was furious...fearful of hearing excuse after excuse...now it was my turn and he wasn't very happy...

I'm here to volunteer sir...

The small angry man behind the desk looked up at me for the first time...and as he did so...his whole personality seemed to change...

No invitation to sit was offered...however...he then asked me why I wanted to volunteer?

I want to fight sir...

With that...I was offered any regiment...my choice. Military law had always interested me...so with that...my call-up papers for the Military Police were signed...there and then...with basic training to begin six weeks later...

The commandant looked at me and asked...

Do you think you can kill?

I answered...*Yes...*

He then smiled at me...*We'll see about that. Two years with MPs...Angola...if you reach the rank of lieutenant...and survive...we'll send you to the military academy. Next!*

My future had been determined in a matter of minutes...

Excitement…

The excited anticipation of what was coming for me filled me as I drove back to Johannesburg…

The answer to my question was about to be revealed to me...and I was joyous. Drinking beers behind the wheel...I felt a sense of relief...at last…

I feared what I would have to do...have to do when wearing the uniform of fear...but it would have to be done for me to find the answer…

Why do we hurt each other?

I knew racism was wrong...I voiced racist views...held racist thoughts...yet I knew it was wrong. I was wearing my mask...one of many...behind which lay the truth of me...a truth that sought the answer to my question…

Why do we hurt each other? Why do we hurt ourselves when we hurt another?

My decision to volunteer...I knew that decision would hurt me...even before I arrived in the office of the small angry man. I knew it would hurt because I knew that I would have to do things...have to see things that went against the very essence of me. But it was the only way...so I thought...the only way to find my answer…

What I didn't know then...was that I would indeed seek the answer to my question…

I would seek the answer...but it wasn't to be that way…not that time. One month after volunteering...only weeks short of wearing the uniform...I found myself driving in open countryside with a work colleague. We were miles from nowhere when it happened…

I lost control of the car…

One minute…we were cruising along the long and never-ending tarmac road that dissected the farmlands…next minute…my work colleague was screaming as we careered over to the right hand side…then over to the left…on and off the road…

I did the best that I could to get the wheel back…but it was hopeless…the car was skidding out of control and then I saw what we were hurtling towards…an iron crash barrier that lined the left hand side of the road…

Taking my hands off the wheel…I turned my body away from what was coming…

It's the noise that I will always remember the most…the thunderous sound of metal smashing against metal…it was an explosion that deafened…then everything went black…

I opened my eyes…opened my eyes and saw the blue sky with clouds above me…

Lying on my back…I heard someone crying…crying loudly and saying words that I couldn't understand…it was my Zulu work colleague who had been in the car with me…

Turning my head to the left…I saw him lying not far away…his body covered in blood…clothes torn apart…as he lay trembling in the long grass…

Seeing he was hurt…I tried to move to help him…but I couldn't move…so I looked back up at the sky…

Oh shit…this is serious…oh shit…

The words went over and over in my mind…I knew we were in trouble and I knew that we were out in the middle of nowhere…nowhere and with no-one around…

Then...the strange feeling...

There was a strange feeling coming from the end of my right leg...not pain...just really unusual...like nothing I'd ever felt before...

I tried to sit up...I couldn't...there was no pain...I just couldn't seem to sit up...so I lifted my right leg up into the air to have a look...

It had gone...my foot had gone...

Bone...flesh...ripped skin...all I could see at the end of my leg...

Gently...ever so gently...I lowered my leg and looked upwards to the heavens above me...

Blue sky...white clouds...drifting...peaceful...

I'm going to bleed to death...

My words were real to me...yet no fear...

Looking above as the clouds floated by...I thought of those who loved me...those who I loved...my parents...brother and sister...Jenny...my friends...they would miss me and I would miss them...

There was no fear...nothing. There was no fear because I had been embraced by an overwhelming sense of calmness...at peace with serenity...as I lay in the field...broken and bleeding...

I sensed him...a man...kneeling behind my right shoulder as I lay on my back. There was no-one there...but I knew a man was behind me...I sensed him...

Lift up your leg John. John...lift up your leg!

I did as I was told...I lifted what was left of my leg into the air...

It was an army patrol that found us...my colleague and myself. I was unconscious...my leg in the air...

The man unseen had saved my life…

I didn't bleed to death because I did what he told me to do...

I couldn't breathe…

I couldn't breathe on my own...shock...two days in intensive care on a life support machine…

My body was broken…

When the car hit the crash barrier...it hit the barrier at an angle...the barrier broke...then smashed its way through my door...through the driving compartment...then out through the passenger door...the car sliding down the barrier as it was impaled on the metal…

My foot had been crushed off...so they amputated just below my right knee. Fractured pelvis...fractured skull...lacerations to my face and back...I was lucky to be alive…

My greatest fear when I regained consciousness was that Jenny would no longer want anything to do with me...a man with no leg…

How could I go on...go on with such a disability for the rest of my life? Yet the human spirit rises to these pains...rises above these pains and it didn't take me long to accept my loss and get on with my life…

Jenny made it clear that she was still my girlfriend...she loved me...she wanted to be with me...I was so relieved...she still wanted me...

Friends and family rallied around and I was blessed with support from those who cared from me...those who loved me…

My fears were no more and within a matter of days I was racing around the hospital wards in a wheelchair...spirits high. I was determined to fight on. I was determined to live. In time I would use this pain to mask my real illness...

Two months…

The prognosis was eight weeks in hospital…I was discharged after two…

My recovery was remarkable…

During my stay…my parents visited me every day…

One afternoon…my mother handed me a photograph. It showed me and three other friends all posing for the camera. My mum asked me if I could see anything unusual in the picture? I looked and looked…nothing. Then she pointed something out to me…a small bolt of white light…white light that crossed my leg…across my leg at the exact point where the surgeons had amputated my limb…

The photo had been taken six months before my accident…

I then shared with my mum about the presence I'd felt…the presence of the man who had been kneeling behind me as I lay on the ground. I shared with my mother about being told to raise my leg and of the overwhelming sense of peace that embraced me at that moment…

We just smiled each other and left it at that…there wasn't much more we could say…so we just smiled…

I lost my leg on the 14th of January 1988. The man who couldn't be seen…the presence I'd felt kneeling behind me…the man who told me to raise my leg…I was to meet him many years later…

His name is Thomas and he showed himself to me in April of this year…2011…

Thomas is a quiet man…thoughtful…strong in faith. When he was on his journey in this Eden…he was known as Thomas…Thomas Aquinas…

Thomas knew the truth of Her…the truth of Mary from Magdala…

Faith…

I had faith that I could lead a normal life…and so I did…

Three months were spent on crutches before I received my first artificial limb…

I was in agony…

It hurt me so much…so I threw it away on the first day…but something within me…around me…sensed to me to put it back on and endure the pain…so I did…

Soon…I managed to walk around without the aid of crutches and so I returned to working with the construction company…

The staff were fantastic…I was told that since I lost my leg during working hours…then my job would be safe for life…as long as I wanted…

The managing director at that point was a man named Nigel…a good man…and I will always be grateful for his kind words…words that gave me security and a sense of belonging…of being wanted…

Studying technical drawing…I soon found a niche that I enjoyed within the company…as well as something else…beers after work…

The months and years were to pass…I became very competent in what I did…and at the same time I was drinking quite heavily…

Again…everyone else seemed to be drinking the same amount…but what they didn't know was that following a few beers in the office after work…I was returning home to my parent's house…where I lived in an outside garden flat…a place where I could easily drink a dozen more by myself…

Openly…I seemed happy…but deep within…I felt lost…lost in so many ways…especially regarding the truth of how I lost control of the car…a truth that I am only admitting now…

These lines I write are all about honesty and truth…

For years…until this time…I've shared with others that I don't know how it happened…how I lost control of the car?

Police measured the tyre marks on the road…I hadn't been speeding. My blood was tested…no alcohol. There were no other cars on the road at the time…I hadn't hit anything or anyone…

There were many theories…some encouraged by myself…

Maybe an animal had run out onto the road?

Maybe a person had stepped out onto the road and I swerved to avoid hitting them…upon which…they ran away?

Some kind of mechanical failure?

So many possibilities…but there's always only one truth…always…

My truth of that day is that I lost control of the car because I fell asleep at the wheel…and I was too ashamed to admit it…

Guilt and shame…both of which I carried for twenty two years…

Fear of being honest for fear of reprisal…

Well now I'm being honest…as these pages I compile are all about the truth…the all-important importance of honesty…

It was my fault…I fell asleep at the wheel…and I will do the best that I can to make amends to my colleague who was also hurt…hurt so badly all those years ago…I will do my best to find him and ask for his forgiveness…

Why did I fall asleep? I don't honestly know…I don't remember being tired and I wasn't under the influence of alcohol…

I do know why it happened. It happened because I was not supposed to wear the uniform of fear…Apartheid…it's that simple…

The years passed...

Relationship...work...family...drinking...my priorities for years...priorities that were to change...

Apartheid was in the grip of death throes by the early nineties...the economy was suffering due to sanctions...my redundancy was therefore no surprise to me...

To be honest...my work had lost its appeal and I was grateful for being released from its employment...

With money in my pocket...I made a decision to take a long break and so made my way back to the land of my birth...Scotland...

I met up with my best friend from South Africa...Ian...who had been backpacking across Europe...

Ian...if you're reading these words...I have only one word for you...*sneezing*...

South African mates...we travelled around for months...staying with family and friends. Sightseeing and drinking...from Edinburgh to the Ring of Kerry...Dublin to York...London to Glasgow. Jenny also joined us for a while and many good times where had as we explored new places together...enjoying new experiences...lots of alcohol on my part...

All good things come to an end. Ian returned home to South Africa...Jenny followed several months later after our relationship ended...

Hong Kong my new destination for work...but it only lasted a month as I found no joy working in civil engineering again...

A one way flight back to Glasgow...I stayed with family...and then shortly afterwards...an experience in the centre of the Clydeside city...

So green are the hills that with love touch your face,

As raindrops fall down caress softly like lace,

Your heart from the riverside pulse daybreak new,

Fond memories of old only lost to the few.

Stone skin lit like gold from the circus you reign,

Eyes far to the distance see towers see Lane,

Your liquid of love whispers late in the night,

So warm in embrace welcomed joy and delight.

Yes green are the hills that with love touch your face,

So smile gentle Hope as I walk with your Grace,

As rain falls on riverside dawns daybreak new,

Fond memories of old only lost to the few...

Glasgow…

Glasgow my home...my home no more…

Weathered in the west and in my heart...with smiles she blesses me still with memories so fond…

Once second in the empire...always first to me. West coast harbour home...my west coast harbour home...my journey's beginning…

So beautiful and alive with life...the lives of the people who smile...laughing eyes that welcome all to the city of friends...

Tears well up within me now as I write these words…

My home she was...my home she may never be again. She held me close...close like a mother holds one so young…

So young I was when she took me in her friendly embrace and steered me on the path that brought me here...to this place so far away...the place where these words need to be written...words of a boy from Glasgow...

Glasgow…

My intention was only a few months…

My plan was to stay for only a short time...then destiny took my hand and edged me onto my new journey...

I met family who had been lost to me for so long...so long yet they welcomed me into their homes...into their hearts…

Those early days would see me walking the wet and windy city streets in awe of the vibrancy all around me…

Feeling like a child I would simply wander alone...exploring a culture so new...so friendly…so alive...so wet...

So friendly the city was to me...smiles and laughter for me from those who barely knew me...from those who knew me not…

Alive with life and love for life along the side of Clyde...the river that gave birth to something unique...something so very special…

Glasgow...heaven in the rain...

It was on day like this that I found myself walking near the street of Hope...when I simply stopped and stood still…

Looking across the street...I saw a large grey building...the feeling within me so very powerful...drawn towards taking a closer look…

As I approached...I looked up and saw a large blue thistle in blue...below the words...Scottish Television…

I simply stood and gazed at the sign above me...my body seemed to be on full charge...powerful as something sensed to me that this place would play a part...such an important part in my life to come…

I made a decision to be guided by my sense...

One phone call…

One phone call to the number advertised in a local newspaper and I found myself doing voluntary work for a media organisation…

Community Service Volunteers… providing training in media skills for those aspiring to work in the industry…including job placements with Scottish Television…

I took my opportunity and volunteered…and within several months…the studios called…looking for people…volunteers with degrees. With no letters following my name…yet with a profound sense of knowing that I could do well in the industry…my words were dishonest on my application form…

The interview went very well…so well that I was offered a placement for work experience with no pay…

Working for free wasn't a problem for me…it was with gratitude that I accepted the offer…and so I found myself in the very studios…the very building that drew me towards it…that wet and windy day…

1993…my whole life was about to change…

My role was audience researcher for a new talk show…hosted by a young STV starlet…

By this time…I was living in a run-down flat in a town called Clydebank…not far from the home where I made my first steps as a boy…

With very little money…I was determined to work as hard as I could to make a name for myself at the studios. With very little money…a saving grace was free meals in the company canteen…allowing me to eat once a day…though there was always money to be had for the occasional pint of beer after work…always a few pennies for that…

It was tough…but I'd found my love…media…

I made an impression…

The show came to an end after a few months and I was offered paid work...not much...but again I was grateful as it afforded me the opportunity to be where I wanted to be…

By the end of 1994...I found myself finding audiences for a politics discussion show. I loved it and made many new friends within and outwith the department. You know who you are...I'm smiling now...

So many great friendships were forged in those early days at STV...so many great friendships now lost...

It makes me sad because these friendships lost are all my fault. The explanation follows soon...but what I will say...is that I will make my amends to those who I hurt...my friends who I drifted from. They mean so much to me...always have done...always will...tears well up within me now. Scottish Television gave me so much during those early times...with invaluable experience in programme production at the top of the list. Working in the politics office...I was soon given videotape to cut...edit suite experience...precious for me in embracing my newly found creativity…

A creative environment...creative mind-sets...wonderful people from all backgrounds and cultures...all colours...my views on race became healthy...I embraced the change and embraced the wrong that Apartheid was...

Once the working day was done...a quick beer or two...then the bus journey home. With little money for heating...my flat was always cold and so I would just lie down on the mattress on the living room floor...watching television...wrapped in blankets...happy that another day in my new job had gone well and looking forward to what lay ahead in the day to come. I sensed that I'd made it in my life...I had a purpose...

On the move...

I was on the move within the endless corridors at STV...

So much experience was to be had...I wanted it all...as much as I could learn and the opportunity to do so. These opportunities came. From politics to undercover work...then documentary research...my confidence was growing...

To say I loved my job would be an understatement...so much experience...experience gained courtesy of the loveliest people who I've ever met...people like me...creative and caring...hard working and funny...they gave me so much and I miss them dearly...I miss my friends...

Many friendly nights were spent in the local pub...directly opposite the main entrance to the studios...

These friendly nights of drinking after work were to become more and more. A wage increase and pension money from South Africa saw me with a healthy bank balance in 1995...so many friendly nights with work colleagues were enjoyed...

My drinking increased and it became normal for me to spend the whole evening at the bar...then buy twelve more to take home with me...

More money also meant that I could afford to move into a nicer flat...Govan on the Southside became my new home...my new home where I would take the occasional day off just to drink beer...the excuse...my leg was sore...

These days off were rare...my passion was my work...my passion saw me offered a position with Scottish TV's flagship news programme...*Scotland Today*. I joined the journalists as a news assistant...

The newsroom taught me so much about journalism...discipline in meeting deadlines...and it introduced me to drinking alone...

JOHN THOMSON
Scotland Today

The newsroom…

The hub of any broadcaster…exciting and stressful…I loved it…

In my experience…the room of news and enthusiastic drinking went hand-in-hand…fond memories I do have of those times   despite the final outcome…the outcome that saw me sit in sheer   terror during my final detox so many years later…

Starting at the bottom…I printed off the scripts for the bulletins and the main lunchtime and teatime programmes. Then…after a short while…I was asked to do voice reports…followed then by covering stories as a reporter…then producing the news bulletins which were broadcast throughout the day…

I learned from the best…men and women who showed me how it was done…who then watched as I went and did it myself…as I do now…

I'm crying again…tears are streaming down my face as I see their faces…all the people who I had the pleasure of working with…my friends…my friends who I would lose because of my illness…would lose because of me…

I need to carry on…

Tears or no tears…I need to carry on with these words because I do have a deadline and I will meet my deadline…

I can't stop crying…it hurts so much as I write this and I don't know why? I had no idea it would be this difficult to write about this…about me…about my friends and about a life I thought I'd left behind…

Please don't get me wrong…I'm so grateful to be alive…to be where I am at this point in my life…my new life with new friends…

I don't know why I'm crying. I just miss my friends…my friends from home…my friends from Glasgow…

So grateful and so humbled I am right now. Gratitude and humility I feel for where I am at this very moment in time…this time in my life. This beauty I see all around me gives me so much hope…hope not just for me…hope for all of us…hope for you…

So many friends I lost…but I would do it all again…go through it all just so that I could be at this point in my life with this new vision of hope…

If my guides in spirit told me that I would…for whatever reason…have to go through it all again…all the madness…I gladly would…

The tears run quietly down my face as I sit alone in my room…in my room where I write these words for you…please be patient…there's so much more to come…I mustn't get caught up in me…

I just need to say one thing…value what is most precious in your life…loved ones and friends. Never let them go…hold onto them dear…for it's those who we hold dear who are valuable…they are what's most precious in life…

Never let them go…hold them close and never let them go…x

Isolation…

It was when I started working shifts in the newsroom that I drank a lot on my own…

No more nine-to-five…my working day was out of sync with pub opening times…so I began my isolation…alone with my illness…

Drinking with my friends had lost its appeal…deep down I knew that all I really wanted to do was loose myself in alcohol…so whenever I could do this…I did it…

Beginning an afternoon shift…it wasn't unusual for me to have a few beers before heading into the studios…a habit that was to become a need…

My first experience of withdrawal occurred one afternoon while I was writing a news bulletin. One moment I was fine…the next…I suddenly became panicky…anxious…unable to stop shaking…

The journalist overseeing the programme approached me and asked me if I was ok? I told him I wasn't. He suggested I grab my jacket and head straight home…nowhere else…straight home…

Mike taught me so much…fond memories I have of working with him…a gifted journalist and a caring man. I think he knew what was happening to me when he said…

Remember…go straight home John…straight home…

Departing through the main entrance…I walked into the darkness that late afternoons present in the winter months in Scotland…

Rain falling softly…seen through the light of the streetlamps above…I turned up the collar of my jacket with the intention of going straight home…

I couldn't stop shaking. I had no idea why…

Fifty yards…

Stepping off the bus…it was fifty yards to the entrance to my flat…

The shaking had become worse…then I saw my local pub…only a few yards away…so I just walked in…

I had no idea that I was going into withdrawal…I just thought I needed something to calm me down…

Ordering a pint of lager…I stood anxiously…anxiously waiting for the barmaid to return with my drink…

My hands were shaking uncontrollably in my jacket pockets when she placed it on the counter in front of me. I waited for her to turn and walk away…then leaned forward and sucked as much beer as I could into my mouth…

Then I did it again…

Somehow…I managed to hold the glass and drink the whole lot at once…hands trembling…liquid splashing all over me…

I had no idea what was happening…but within ten or twenty minutes…within three drinks…the shaking had stopped…

Feeling cured of whatever had been ailing me…I wandered home after a few more pints…buying more alcohol on the way…

My withdrawals from alcohol weren't many…only because I kept drinking whenever I could…whenever I felt that I needed to…

This need occurred every day…so every day I drank alcohol…still none the wiser as to just how ill I was becoming….just how ill I was. After years of drinking on a daily basis…my tolerance to alcohol had become so high…

But a tolerance for so much more was on its way…

So much more…

The sports department…

One of the news producers approached me with an offer...the sports department was looking for an assistant producer...he thought it would be a good move for me…

Paul told me that he could see a very creative side to my production skills...that the move to sport would offer me a more suited platform to explore my creativity...

I agreed…

With my new title as assistant producer...I entered the world of sport...or should I say...football…

From a journalistic point of view...I didn't have a clue. Celtic and Rangers had only ever provoked an interest from me...the rest were unknown…

I made the transition nonetheless and learned as much as I could...as quickly as I could. I entered the sports office in August 1997...and it was from the same department that I stood down from my career in broadcasting...nine years later…due to my illness...

So much happened for me and to me during my time with sport. It was emotional for me earlier when writing about friends lost in the newsroom...many of my colleagues in the sports department were to become like brothers and sisters to me…

So a new beginning for me once again...and it was with this new beginning that I met her. We met in a dingy smoke-filled bar during a STV function...a beautiful young woman who left me mesmerised...a beautiful young woman who would one day say *I do* as we looked lovingly into each others' eyes…

The tears come again...

Kirsty...

We met and we fell in love...

Love at first sight...I'd always been curious...then I met Kirsty and my curiosity was answered...it does happen...

Beautiful...caring...a loving friend to those close to her...

My colleague had warned her beforehand...

Don't go near him...he's an alcoholic and he's a shagger!

That night when we met...Kirsty asked me if the allegations were true? Laughing out loud...I replied...

Me? An alcoholic?!?

We both burst out laughing and that was that...the beginning of a togetherness that would last for nine years...

Those early days...they bring a smile to me now...a smile to ease the tears. Those memories...so long ago yet so clear...our favourite restaurant...then holding hands as we dashed home in the rain...talking and laughing...drenched to the bone...

I fell in love...from the moment I met her...I fell in love...

Six months were to pass and we moved in together. We were happy...both of us had great jobs...the world was opening up for us...a future...

It all seems so long ago now...yet I think of her from time to time. I will always love her...always did...always will. I know we'll never be together again...I only really accepted that just after my treatment at Broadway...

My acceptance came when I asked her for her forgiveness...my acceptance came with her answer...*I forgave you a long time ago....*

With that...I broke down. I broke down and let her go...

We had held each other for so long…

The years passed and I became part of her family…Kirsty's parents welcomed me with open arms…

John and myself became close and I knew he cared very much for me…a father figure…always making sure that I had what I needed…a very giving and generous man…

But it was Mary with whom I was to develop a very special relationship …very special…

A kind and compassionate woman…a woman who had a special gift with children. Mary was a retired schoolteacher when we met…a very rare soul…an old soul…wise to the world and with an endless amount of love to give…especially to young people…

It's with fondness and love that I remember Mary as my *Greenock Mum.* Sometimes…when we looked into each other's eyes…it was as if we were looking into each other's souls and it blessed me with a sense of peace…

Greenock…the port town to the west of Glasgow…a place where I would spend many fond times with my new family. John…Mary…Kirsty…and her sister Rhona. Warm and loving…especially on Sundays when we would gather for one of John's special dinner's…a man of the sea…the former ship's pilot had been no stranger to a galley kitchen or two…his cooking was always first-class…like his long and adventurous career on the high seas…

We were close…we were all so very close…

Sometimes…when I'm troubled or looking for some guidance…I talk to my Greenock mum. I know she's with me…I know she's with all of us. She told me once that I needed to let go of the past…she's always close…I feel her with me now as the tears well up again…

I hurt myself the most…

My hurting of others was imminent...my hurting of myself was well underway…so much hurt was to come...

The new millennium...new beginnings for all...a new beginning for me as a highly functioning alcoholic…alcoholic and bulimic...

I drank every day...lunchtime...after work...at home...

Once our evening meal was done...I would go into the bathroom and force myself to be sick...so that the alcohol could enter my bloodstream quickly. Needless to say...I never really drank much when eating...but I did upon returning to the table...

Our days off work were different…

Kirsty would say goodbye in the morning...once gone...I would run to the corner shop where I would buy two bottles of wine and six large beers…

One bottle of wine would be hidden behind the curtain in the lounge...the rest I would drink by myself...then pass out for a few hours before she returned home…

Some wine shared in the evening...Kirsty would then retire to bed...

I would say that I would join her shortly...then from behind the curtain would come the hidden bottle...it was drunk within a minute…

And so it went on…and on…

No-one knew what was happening...I didn't know what was happening. I know it probably sounds strange...I new something was wrong...but that something eluded me for so long…

Highly functioning...my tolerance was growing. A highly functioning alcoholic...still functioning in a very stressful career...

Growth…

We were growing together and growing in life as time passed…

Our careers were going so well…Kirsty an account manager with a respected sports events marketing company in Glasgow…me with a number of years behind me in the sports department and a promotion to producer…

We talked of having a baby…a wee one…Amy or Ailee for a little girl…Jack for a little boy…

Our new home was bought in 1999…a brand new city flat in a refurbished Victorian building…we were a couple on the move. From the outside…our life looked great…and it was. But deep within me…I was struggling…

The feeling of being different…feeling lost…not worthy of happiness…that feeling had always been with me and continued to be so despite my new-found success in life…

Feeling not worthy for feeling different…that had also taken its hold…a hold that had gripped me for as long as I could remember…

Certain events from the past began creeping up on me…the parking garage with the woman…the car accident…lying broken and   bleeding in a field…the feeling of being alone…of being different…the sense that I didn't deserve to live…didn't deserve a life. The joker on the outside…terrified deep within…always a mask I wore so that no-one could see in…see the real me. It was the real me that I was afraid of…because the real me was a grown man in fear…a young and frightened boy on the inside…a funny successful man on the outside…

Fear…fear of so much…so much more than I had feared as a young boy…

Please don't let me see…I don't want to see…

Still the sense of being watched…

It had never really left me…it just seemed to me that I was more aware of the   feeling when I was a young boy…

As a grown man…I would introduce logical explanations to myself…but really…I knew there was something…

I've always believed in that something…always believed…but it had always scared me…

The feeling of being watched heightened around this time…the time in our new home…

There had been times in the past…when asleep…that I felt myself leave my body…yet still feeling awake…

This sensation elevated and started to become something more…

In the early hours of one morning…I awoke to find myself standing in our bedroom…looking down on myself and my love as we lay sleeping…

This experience happened several times…and I remember knowing that I could leave the room if I wanted to…but fear prevented me from doing so…

One night…it happened again…and I found the courage to leave our bedroom. I walked down the long hallway and entered the large living area. I saw three young women…all dressed in Victorian clothing…sitting at our dining room table. They were smiling at me. I turned and then saw a tall figure…a man…wearing dark clothes from the same period…a tall top hat…

Looking at the smiling women…I said…*I'm John.*

Still smiling…they replied…*We know who you are…*

The room felt warm…warm and without fear. It would be exactly ten years before I was to find out who they were…

So much warmth…

We shared many evenings together in our new home…

Dinner and wine...we would sit and share about work...our plans for the future...

One evening...Kirsty shared her fear with me...a fear that her mum would never see one of her daughters walking down the aisle…

Mary had been unwell for some time...but not life-threatening...

I knew that I loved Kirsty...I knew that I wanted to be with her for the rest of my life….so I stood up and walked over to where she was standing...knelt down on one knee. I asked...and she said...

Yes…

We both cried…tears of love for one another...tears of love for my Greenock mum…

We were married in Glasgow in 2002...a glorious day in a wonderful venue opposite the city's stunning Cathedral…

The morning of the wedding...I walked alone and into the ancient place of worship and wandered in silence amid the high alters of stone…

Something within me told me to go...so I went...I went and found serenity within the heart of the greatness that lay within its granite walls…

After some time...I departed to get ready for our big day...

There was very little fear within me that morning...I was at peace in knowing I was about to marry my true love...marry my true love under the loving gaze of the city's great place of faith…

My belief was to come...in time it would hold me...hold me when I needed to be held...

Beautiful...

My bride was beautiful and so was our day...

It all seemed to fly by in a haze...so many people...people who loved us...people there for us as we exchanged our vows and promised forever...

Mr and Mrs Thomson...

Our honeymoon saw us travel to the country where I grew as a boy...South Africa...

We did it all...Cape Town...Zululand...Victoria Falls on the border with Zambia and Zimbabwe...

Surrounded by beauty...in the embrace of my new wife...in the tightening grip of my illness...

Any excuse to sneak away...away for a quick dash into a bar to knock back drink after drink...then return to Kirsty...behaving as if nothing had happened. My new wife...she didn't know...

It was a skill that I mastered well...dishonesty...dishonest with myself and those who loved me...

Even at this point...I had no idea what was happening to me. All I knew was that I needed to drink...needed to...needed to take alcohol to numb something within me...

For so long...I'd felt as if I was standing watch...standing watch in a tower so high...a tower from which I could see a great storm approaching on the distant horizon...

As I stood and watched the storm approach...my fear would build...knowing full well that I was going to feel the full force of something terrible...

The storm hit in 2003…

My career was my success…

I produced many sports programmes and they were successful…

Mixing with famous faces from the football world…wining and dining …I held a privileged position within Scottish Television…

Premiership football…European football…Murrayfield…the home of Scotland's First XV…

So I was asked to produce Rugby World Cup coverage from Australia…

I was thirty five years old…

The hours were long and the work was stressful. I was feeling the strain…strain not from work…strain from living a double life…

My illness was now becoming chronic…

Our home was littered with hiding places. Vodka in washed-out shampoo bottles so that I could drink when getting ready for work. Two small bottles of wine bought on the way into the office…breakfast. Pints of lager at lunchtime. The same during the afternoon…with no-one knowing. Drinks after work. Walking home…I would buy something for our evening meal…including four bottles of wine. One would be drunk in the toilets of the food store. One would be drunk in an alleyway not far from our home. Two bottles remained…one for dinner with my wife…the final bottle hidden in my briefcase…then stashed somewhere to be drunk in the early hours of the morning…

Day after day after day…it went on for months…but it had to end…

Despite this…my job of producing the World Cup was a success. We came off air and headed to the nearest pub to celebrate…

The storm I'd been waiting for had arrived…the first storm…

I felt calm…

I felt calm as I laughed and joked with my colleagues…my friends…as we all congratulated each other on jobs well done…

There was a great sense of relief for me…hard work…so hard with long hours…but I'd managed to get it done…

I had two pints of lager and then bid my friends farewell…

Early November…clear and cold…I walked straight to a nearby shop…a shop so near where I bought two large bottles of vodka…

Then to a nearby hotel…a room…a room where I opened the first bottle…

Five days were to pass…five days of uncontrollable tears…drinking…then blackout…regaining consciousness…then leaving the room to buy more alcohol…

Frantically searching…my friends couldn't find me…

The storm had arrived…

Crawling around in my room…it seemed as if the very essence of me was being ripped apart. Flashbacks to times gone by…times of fear…times of dark places and open highways…fear of everything…everything including life…fear of all…fear of me and fear of not knowing what was wrong…

Somehow…I managed to find my way home…

Five days had passed…

Kirsty opened the door…we looked at each other…her eyes were wide with fear too…filled with fear and tears…

I started to cry…the said…

I think there's something wrong with me…

She held me close and we both cried together…

My drinking was shared…

We sat and I told her everything…shared with her where the hiding places were…shared with her how much I'd been drinking every day…

She was stunned…but held it together…she held her composure because I shared with her my desire to stop…

That night…we lay in the dark and she held me close…held me close as the withdrawal began…held me closer when my body shook uncontrollably…

Kirsty never did me any harm…she always looked out for me and she always wanted the very best for me…she wanted the best for me because she loved me…a love which I returned to her…but it was a love that was powerless over my illness…

The morning awakened and my wife departed for Greenock to share everything with her parents. I promised that I would be okay…okay on my own…I promised…

My promise lasted no more than ten minutes once she'd gone…

The walk to the store and back took me twenty minutes…but twenty minutes was too long…half of the bottle of vodka was swallowed as I stood on the pavement…on the pavement outside the shop…

Hours later…when Kirsty returned from Greenock…I was delirious…ranting about how there were people in our home…people she couldn't see…people who I could see…

My best friend Marcus was called and he helped to calm me down while the police and ambulance crew made their way to help me…

My first hospital admission was about to begin…Marcus helped us so much that night in keeping me calm…I miss my friend…

I miss my best friend…

Once again...tears...

Once again the tears well up within me as I write of someone else who I love...someone else who I've lost...

Marcus...

There's no-one else like him...never has been...never will be...

He stood by my side on the day I took my vows. He stood by my side when we went to Murrayfield to watch Scotland play rugby. He stood by my side when we enjoyed barbecues together. He stood by my side when he pulled me out of my car...slumped in the seat. Even then then he stood by my side...

My tears they flow once again as I remember the man who will always be my best friend...my best friend he will always be...even if I never see him again. I pray I do...

Marcus...my mate...he stood by me through the laughter...through the horror...

If God were to grant me another brother...I would ask for Marcus...

One day I hope to meet him again...meet him again to ask for his forgiveness....forgiveness for abusing his love for me...abuse that saw me let him go...a friendship lost when I isolated myself from him...

Marcus sat with me that night and helped me to find calm...always by my side when I found myself lost...

My heart is sore as I write these words...these words for a man who I love...love like a brother...the father of my Godson...

Glasgow comes to me soon I hope...soon I hope to make my amends to many...especially Marcus...

Marcus will be one of the first of the many...with my God willing...

The Western Infirmary...

My first hospital admission for alcohol abuse lasted two weeks…

The Western Infirmary sits in the middle of the city's West End...adjacent to Glasgow University...bustling with pubs and shops...

My second night...I managed to sneak away from the ward for twenty minutes to buy a bottle of vodka...drink it...then return calmly as if nothing was wrong…

The hallucinations followed shortly after…not violent...but terrible to witness for others in the ward...

A chronic alcoholic in the grip of the most misunderstood illness in the world...even the nurses were shocked by my behaviour…

Fourteen days later...my body was detoxed and I was allowed to go home. I was signed off from work with a *stress related illness*…

Anti-depressants were prescribed...as well as a tablet which had to be taken daily...a tablet to stop me from drinking anything alcoholic. If I did drink...then I would be violently ill. I was warned…

Three months off sick from work...I managed to build myself up again. I ate healthily...went to the gym every day...took my medication...began to feel so much better...began to feel alive again…

I was also diagnosed as suffering with post-traumatic stress disorder...as well as a bipolar mood disorder…

These diagnoses were welcomed by me. At last...a remedy for my ills…

Hope was building within me and I became strong again. My family and friends had gathered around me...supporting me through this difficult time...supporting me with love...

Then we lost our love...

Mary became seriously ill...

My Greenock mum was diagnosed with breast cancer. The family was distraught as Mary had been ill for some time...now cancer...

Her spirits remained high...remained strong even when they took that part away...

Autumn 2004...

Mary met her end...at home...with John and Kirsty and Rhona at her bedside. My Greenock Mum was with her husband and her daughters when she ended her journey in this Eden. They held her close as she passed in peace...

Standing in the kitchen...I felt my Greenock mum leave us...

She stayed with us that night...that night as I lay on the floor...sensing that she was still with us...her love for us holding us as we mourned her loss...

For some reason...no tears came for me when Mary passed...my tears for my Greenock mum fall softly for her now as I write these words...so many tears fall softly now...fall gently for a woman who I love dearly...

Mary isn't far away...her love for us is all around us...her love for us I see. My Greenock mum has gone home...then from time to time...she looks in on us to offer a hand of love...and hand that touches me now...

The love of Mary...the love of so many others...around me...around all of us...their love I see now...

For me...life after death doesn't exist...I like to think of it as life after life...

My Greenock mum gave me a gift...she blessed me with knowing her...

I said goodbye to love...

Fourteen months after Mary's passing...I said goodbye to my wife...

Two years had passed since my hospital admission...twenty four months of getting strong...only to think that I was strong enough to control my drinking...

Kirsty told me I couldn't...

And then I said something that hurt her terribly...terribly dishonest and something that would hurt me too...

In that moment...I became angry...I became angry because I was afraid...my fear of the truth in she was saying...

With fear I looked at my wife...the beautiful woman who loved me and only wanted the best for me...and said...

I do love you...but I'm not in love with you...

As my words were heard...I saw her pain...

Fear within words causes so much damage between people...my words of damage were to hurt me too in the months to come...

I packed my bags and drove to Gleneagles where I got drunk...

Now I had reached the beginning of the end...the end of everything that I had aspired to...worked so hard for...

Standing on the watchtower so high...the storm I saw heading towards me was bigger than the one before...bigger than the storm that had thrown me into my first hospital admission...

Chronic...progressive...life-threatening illness...

The storm had arrived...the storm was angry...the storm was my own fear...

Tempestuous were the months to come...

My farewell...

My farewell to the city I loved...2006...twelve months I spent alone in my own madness...alone with my illness...

A garden flat in the city's West End was to be my home for those twelve months...one year during which time I nearly drank myself to death...

So desperate and so alone...

My isolation from those who loved me...from the world...was part of my illness...my isolation from life...

All I wanted to do...needed to do...was drink myself into oblivion at every waking moment...as every waking moment was what I feared the most...

Numbness...blackout...those were my desires now...

My first admission into a psychiatric ward...a two week detox...then discharge...only to relapse again and again. The detoxes were many that year...

It went on and on...not even the continued and caring help of a community psychiatric nurse could help me...no-one and nothing could help me...

Post-traumatic stress...bipolar mood disorder...simply conditions that I'd welcomed...anything...just please don't label me an alcoholic. But that was the truth of me then...a man filled with fear of everything...including what people thought of me. So what did they think of me? What did people think of me when they saw me stumbling along Byres Road...unwashed...dirty clothes...smelling of urine...staggering to buy bottle after bottle of the only thing that I could think of...the only thing that mattered to me...

Irony can be beautiful...irony can be tragic...

The final tragedy…

The final tragedy almost took place on Christmas Eve of that year…

Twelve months of hell…yet somehow still alive…

But life for me was lost to my state of mind…

My abuse of myself had to end at some point…so I decided to do it myself…

24 December 2006…

Late on that festive afternoon…I staggered through the sea of smiling faces…jolly faces rushing around on the West End streets…last minute shopping amid the anticipation of the celebration that was imminent…

I stumbled into the shop and barely managed to mumble what it was that I needed…

One final bottle of vodka…

Returning to my stinking mess…my home…I realised that I'd lost my keys. I made a decision to end it all by simple hiding in the alleyway…to fall asleep in the cold. Then…I decided to just break into my flat…so I picked up a brick and staggered towards my front door…hurling the stone as I approached the large window next to the doorway…

The glass exploded. I looked around to see if anyone had noticed…no-one had…so I struggled on and desperately pulled myself through the window with the final pockets of strength that I had left. Landing on my back in the sitting room…I looked down and saw the blood covering my right hand…peering closer…I saw that the top of my middle finger had been cut off. It didn't bother me. I just sat and looked at it for a while…then opened the bottle of vodka…

I should never have been here...

Those were the words that repeated over and over in my mind as I sat mindless...bleeding...taking huge gulps from the bottle...

I don't belong in this world. Why did I have to come here?

The words were now joined by tears as I sat and wept at the state of myself...what my life had become...my life in this world...a world where I'd felt like I never belonged...

Why did I have to come here?

The same words...over and over...crying as I thought of my family...my wife...my friends...

Sitting on the sofa...a sofa covered in broken glass...I wrote a message for my parents on my mobile phone. I told them how sorry I was for all the hurt I'd caused them. I told them to tell Kirsty that I loved her so much...so much...and that I was so sorry for what I had done to her...said to her. I told them to tell my brother and sister that I loved them too...and that I would see them all again one day...one day in the place where we go at the end. I told my parents that I was so sorry...

The broken glass covered the chair...

I gulped down the rest of the vodka and waited for a short while...some time for the alcohol to take effect...

The numbness began...calming...I felt at peace...

The first cuts to my wrist were shallow...testing my pain barrier...no pain...

I'm so sorry...

My final words as I closed my eyes and ripped the broken glass across my left wrist...

Drifting…

I felt myself drifting slowly away as life poured from me…

A sense of nothingness as the icy winter wind blew against the back of my head…behind me the broken window that now invited the cold Christmas air to wrap me in its chilled embrace…

Sobbing softly to myself…I bent over and looked down upon the floor…my boots sitting amid the dark puddle of life that was growing as every second passed…

Wanting to lie down…I staggered to my feet and avoided looking down again…careful not to slip and fall into what was once inside of me…

I was drifting…drifting away as I held onto the walls for support…I could feel myself drifting further and further away…

Somehow…I managed to pull myself up the stairs and collapsed onto my stinking bed…

The flat had been beautiful when I moved in. During times of sobriety…I'd kept the place really tidy…proud of my new home and proud of my efforts at staying sober…

The bed was a mess when I collapsed onto it…

Lying on my front…I folded my arms beneath the pillows…then realising that my blood would make a terrible mess on the sheets…I moved onto my left side so that my arm could hang over the side of the bed…to avoid staining the bed linen…

That was my only thought as I drifted off…drifted away…

24 December 2006…the eve of giving…the day I decided to take myself away from life so that I would stop hurting others. I decided it was better to hurt myself instead…

Darkness…

I awoke in the darkness of that early Christmas morning…

The room was black and still as I opened my eyes…

Lying in the dark...it took me a while to come to terms with what I was sensing...I was alive…

Sitting up so slowly on the bed...I saw the light from stairwell shine up and into the room...so I stumbled towards the light…

As I moved closer to the stairwell...I began to see the blood on the walls...bloody handprints and smears...it was everywhere…

Struggling with the stairs...I managed to cling onto the bannister and made my way down and into the main room...the room where I had hurt myself…

The floor was awash with a black sticky mess...the sofa was too...so much blood...so much…

I looked down at my wrist and saw the gaping hole...flesh torn apart and exposing what shouldn't be exposed in that way...

Collapsing onto the floor...I just sat in disbelief for an unknown amount of time...I couldn't believe I was alive…

The room was so cold...so very cold with the window broken...I was freezing and there was no heating available. Somehow...there was a small amount of hot water...so I had a bath and soaked my arm…

Afterwards...naked...I just sat in the icy and bloody living room...shivering…

I must have gone into shock…

I just sat still...in the middle of the room...waiting…

Nothing happened...the room got colder...I was terrified...

No-one came…

No-one came because no-one knew. I didn't want to call anyone and spoil their Christmas Day…

I crawled back up to my room…curled up so cold beneath my covers…freezing. My heart was pounding…racing…

Please let me have a heart attack…please end me now…

My plea went unanswered…then something…

Lying in the darkness…I became aware of words…words not from me…

They come for you soon…

As I heard the words…the strange words in my mind…it seemed I could see three figures approaching from within the darkness. The figures were   coming from light…the figures were wearing robes…

The words and the figures gave me a new strength…a new strength as I lay in the darkness. Then…my own words…

I'm not going yet…I'm not ready…I want to live…

With those words…my words…I pulled myself out of the bed and once again made my way back downstairs. Struggling alone in the freezing room…the pain in my arm began and my withdrawal was well underway…

My new resolve didn't last long in my desperate state. Shivering…in fear…in pain…withdrawal…I took a sheet from my bed…then looked for a place to suspend myself…

There was nowhere to hang…so I crawled into the kitchen and closed the door…forcing a towel into the gap at the bottom so that none would escape. The gas was turned on. I lay down in the middle of the floor…I took deep breaths…

Then...more strange words...

This isn't the time...not like this...you must be strong...

The words gave me strength...I turned off the gas and returned to sitting alone in the front room...

I sat alone...in the cold...for the whole of Christmas Day 2006. I sat alone and didn't call anyone because I didn't want to upset anyone on that special day...a day when families come together to rejoice and have fun...to give thanks to loved ones...

I sat alone until the following day...the day of St Stephen...

My dear friend Marcus arrived to help me...take me away from the place of madness...my madness...

I never returned...

Glasgow my home...

Glasgow my home no more...

Relapse...

Three years of relapse after relapse was to follow...

Marcus had driven me south to be with my parents...their home on the east coast of England...

My poor mum and dad were devastated at what I'd become. They did their very best for me but it must have been soul-destroying for them to witness my downfall...

Once a man who had it all...wife...home...career...future...all slipping away...

I attended a twelve week drug and alcohol course to help me with my substance abuse...but that began to fall apart towards the end of the three months...

I met a local girl and it was to be a new relationship for me. We lasted three years together...three years of the same abuse that I had inflicted on Kirsty...relapse...hiding bottles...periods of sobriety...old behaviours over and over again...

A new addiction was to grip me...painkillers...

Times when I abstained from alcohol were times when I would swallow dangerous amounts of codeine-based pills...anything to change the way I felt...a release from myself and from life...

The warning on the box would state no more than eight tablets per day...I was swallowing one hundred...

The hurt to myself and others continued...so many lies...no-one knew what I was doing...no-one knew the real me...I didn't know the real me...

The real me was a man in fear...

Masks…

My masks were many…coloured with confidence…

No-one really knew me…not even me. I portrayed myself as a man confident…funny…a leader. But the reality of me was a man filled with fear…fearful of everything and everyone…even myself…

I feared me because I had no idea who I truly was or what my purpose was in this life…in this Eden. Fearful and confused…I created so many masks from which I could hide behind…from where I could perform my own masquerade for others on a daily basis. Yet deep down inside…I was just a fearfully sad and lonely man…lost to himself and to the world…

With no faith in myself or who I was…I found it easy to hurt myself…oblivious to the consequences of my actions. This would have been acceptable if I'd limited the hurt to myself. But the reality was that I didn't just hurt myself…I hurt those who I loved and cared for too…those who loved and cared for me…

I was a man lost. I took from so many and gave nothing in return…with the exception of hurt. I wasn't a bad person…but I did bad things…especially the hurt of women…

There had been so many women in my life…in the life of a man who craved the attention of the opposite sex. I'm not an attractive man…but I can be a charming man…and this charm I used on many occasions to satisfy my own selfish desires…

That was the kind of man I was then…not the man I am now. I've learned that I can change…and change I have. The hurt of this man to himself is now no more. The hurt of this man to others is now no more. Heaven exists within every human being. I have no right to hurt to hurt another soul…to hurt Heaven…

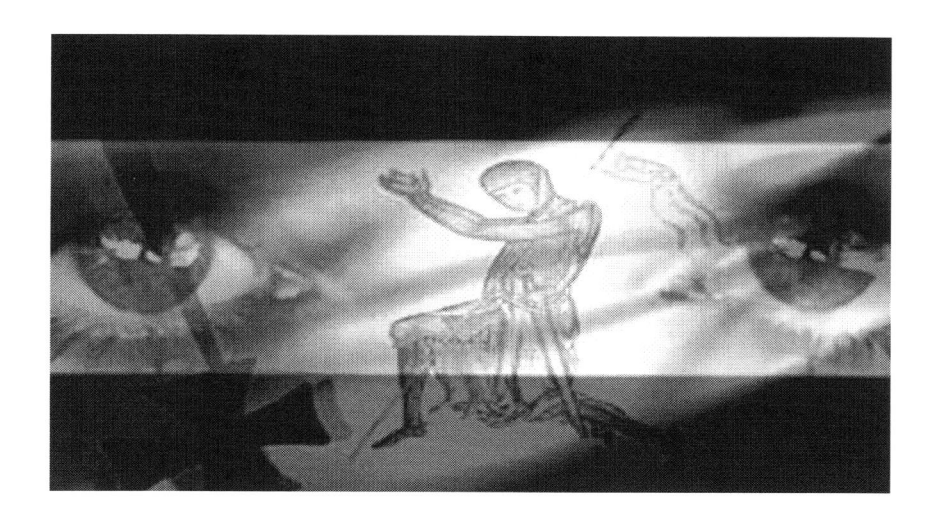

I made a promise to Her…

The Magdalene has heard my promise. My vow to her is that I will never hurt another soul ever again. My words to her were honest and true. For the rest of my days…I will never hurt another…especially a woman…

I can change…I have changed. As man and a human being…I can change and stop the hurt…hurt to myself and hurt to others. With honesty…open-mindedness and willingness…I can make a difference…

My promise is to a woman of love and forgiveness…a woman who once carried this message so long ago. It was my time in *The Place of Miracles* that guided me towards the truth…the Truth of Her…and then the Truth of my blessing of Prophecy. Does this sound deranged? Four simple words can confirm the truth of what I experience…*Manila comes for you…*

So much work had to be done before I saw those words. I first had to face my own truth at Broadway Lodge…

Chapter Eight

The Truth of Honesty...

My share of my life was almost done…

I spoke of how Ed had taken me away from the homeless hostel in Ipswich…the room with the window…

My share ended with words of gratitude…so I grateful I was to be at Broadway…so grateful for the help from the staff and especially my peers… people like me…

My share was done…my story of how I ended up at the *Place of Miracles*…

But I hadn't been totally truthful…

During my share…I'd embellished my truth…

I shared with my peers…my new friends…that I'd been to university…that I'd interviewed a certain famous football manager…

It never happened…

My early days at Broadway were guiding me towards honesty…but my defects of character were still very much at large…

My ego…my arrogance…my low self-esteem…my low self-worth…my heightened sense of self…they all dictated some words untrue…

It was early days…my masks remained many…masks that were soon to be removed…

My peers sat in silence…looking at me…I sat feeling uncomfortable…uneasy in knowing that all eyes were on me…vulnerable. Then…my peers began sharing back…identifying…sharing of how they too had suffered…some more terribly than me. It was humbling…humbling for all in the room…it was powerful. People sharing with one another…sharing the truth of our fears…sharing and healing…

It's all about fear for me…

Fear knocked…faith answered…and there was nothing there…

Honesty is my faith…a faith that blesses me with the gift of sight…

The fear I face in my life…is fear I face with the truth. It took me some time to come to terms with this beautiful reality…time that wasn't easy…

Embracing honesty…true honesty…and facing the truth of myself? That was difficult…it remains difficult…it will always be difficult…but it helps me to grow as a human being…

Someone said to me once…

There's honesty…then there's stupidity…

Faith in being honest transcends fear…fear of the consequences of being honest. Faith and honesty go hand in hand…the kind of truth that embraces blind faith…

For me…there isn't anything stupid about that…that's true faith…

My belief in the power of laughter was something I also found again…real and honest and funny…laughing from deep within…

So many times in primary care…I found myself in tears…crying and sobbing…face wet with joy…

Laughter heals…

I'd lost everything…so had all of my peers…yet we laughed so much as the healing was underway…

The lost had found their way to the place…the place where the miracles were happening…

Laughter heals and I healed so much…

The man with smiles was beginning to awaken…

Laughter…

One Saturday evening...I found myself crying with laughter…

Then...all of a sudden...I felt guilty…

You don't deserve to laugh...you've hurt so many people...why are you laughing?

I withdrew from the hilarity and left the room. I headed outside and found the quiet spot at the side of the mansion...a place where we could go and sit on the bench...the bench that overlooked the little waterfall and pond…

Sitting alone on the bench...it was dark and cold. I felt terrible...I sensed the voice within me was true. At that point...I heard an almighty scream...a shriek of terror…

A fellow peer had turned the corner expecting the bench to be empty...only to see a dark figure huddled in the corner...me...

Addicts...we're a sensitive bunch...

Once the screaming had stopped...as well as the swearing...we both looked at each other and began to laugh...uncontrollably…

Another voice within me said...*It's okay to laugh John...*

So laugh I did…

The days were long and the work was hard…it had to be…but so much fun was had at the same time…

It was during my time in primary care that I started writing silly poems…

The evenings blessed me with free time to spend with my peers in the large coffee lounge within the mansion. Coffees and chats…the room was always lively…

Enjoying the atmosphere of smiles with my friends…I would jot down lines of fun…fun that I would share just for a laugh. So many good people…so many good people with wonderful hearts and minds…it was a privilege to know them…to still know them. One of them was Rachel. She hated mornings…so it was best to stay clear…

I saw her one sunny morning…so radiant from afar…

And so I moved towards her…hand reached to meet a star…

She looked just like a Diva…and as I inched more near…

I saw a sparkle in her eyes…and then I felt the fear…

My hand so gently touched hers…hello my name is John…

Oblivious to how she felt…just seconds after dawn…

She looked up and she stared at me…so soft like lovely lace…

And then she kicked me in the nuts and punched me in the face…

I loved those nights…laughing with friends and scribbling silly lines of rhyme…lines I loved to write…

It's a love I embrace to this day…

Chapter Nine

I Fell in Love...

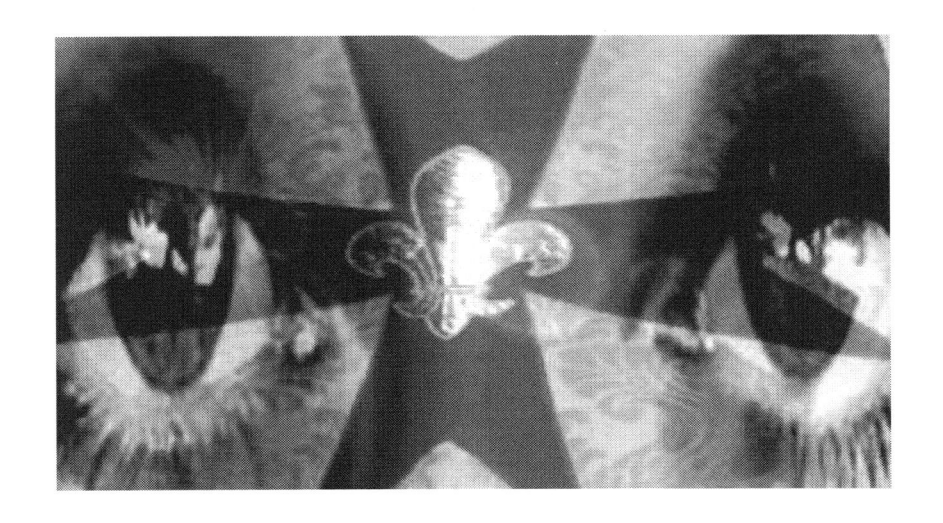

Love so powerful…

I fell in love at *The Place of Miracles.* So beautiful…so kind…so generous…

Her name is Lou…the *Valley Girl…*

I saw her for the first time…not long after my arrival…

She was standing at the main entrance to the old mansion…standing and laughing and smiling…the way that only she can…

It was instant…it was powerful…so powerful as I was drawn to her…

He name is Lou and she is *The Valley Girl…*lines of love in rhyme…

We were to become close as we faced our fears together…together with our peers…all together in a place where Angels dwell…

I believe in Angels…Angels guided me towards a place of healing where Angels helped me to heal…

I believe in Angels…I know this because I've seen them…visions of Hope from where our Truth watches over all of us…

Heaven...

I see Heaven all around me now...Heaven in life...so real in light so white...

Those early days at Broadway blessed me with getting to know her...someone so very special...

Lou was one week ahead of me in the programme and would therefore head back into the world before me...

The times we spent sharing with one another about so many things...our lives...our hopes...our fears...so very special and so very honest...

Whenever she walked into the room...my heart would just start pounding...pounding as I looked around to see if anyone could see that I was smitten...fearful of the implications...

You see...romantic behaviours within the Lodge are stopped very quickly by the staff. It has to be this way...it cannot be allowed to happen because lives are at stake...

The focus has to remain on getting well...not getting amorous with someone else on the programme...

Relationships are the main cause of relapse in recovery...so relationships can kill...relationships do kill...

I fell in love with Lou...I never told her...

My fear of being found out by staff meant that I shared my feelings about her with no-one...not even my counsellor...

The thought of being put on a warning...resulting in not being able to talk with her...that thought I could not bear...

All I wanted to do was hold her...hold her close and tell her that I was falling in love with her. But I never did...I was too afraid...

We shared so much…

We shared so much together…thoughts and feelings…laughter and tears…

So gentle and generous is Lou…so filled with an essence of something so very special…someone so special who I was to know for such a short spell of time…magical times…

Her smile…her voice…the very soul of her…the very essence of her…she had me from the moment I saw her…

So long it has been since we've seen each other…so long this time of fifteen months…

So I never shared with her my true feelings for her…a woman with a man and a child in her life…it didn't feel the right thing to do. I was just so grateful to get to know her and for us to become close together within the old stone walls of a place so special…

For me…angels do dwell within that place so magical…
The Place of Miracles…angels who heal…angels who are healed…

I fell in love with my own angel…someone who I feel so blessed to have known…known for such a short time…

Lou told me that she was returning home once her primary care was complete. I suggested she stay and continue with secondary treatment…a further three months…she decided two months was enough and that she was ready to face the world again…return to her life and her family…

Then…only days before she was due to depart…Lou asked me if I would give her away at her Medallion…an ending ceremony. I was so grateful to be asked…so grateful to be asked by the woman who didn't know that I loved her…

Holding back the tears…I said…*Yes…*

Medallion…

When a peer finishes primary care…a Medallion is held…

With only peers allowed to attend…it's an affirmation by the many for the one…the one who returns to the world having completed the first Five of The Twelve Steps…

For peers by peers…

It's a celebration of eight works of hard work well done…two months of facing fear and getting honest…a long time for anyone who walks through the large wooden doors…straight of the madness of active addiction…

Not many make it…the illness is ever-present…many only last a few weeks…a few days…a few hours…before returning to the nightmare…

Medallion…

We help each other…we affirm each other…addictive personalities bonded by the same experience…strength…and hope…

Two months of hard work is affirmed and a celebration is held. The peer who is leaving asks someone to give them away…to walk them into the large hall and oversee the affirmations.

It was a privilege for me to be asked by Lou…it was with honour that I accepted…it was with love that I gave her away to our peers…then away to the world…

It was a mild October night…clear of sky above the stillness of what had been a beautiful autumnal day. We were all about to say goodbye to someone very special…so I did the best I could to make it very special for her in giving her away…

The room…the lecture hall where my awakening began…a special place for me…a special place for many…

There were many…

The hall was full as primary care was full…

Around thirty peers took their places in a large circle within the room…

Standing outside in the hallway…Lou and me waited for all to be ready within the hall…

I looked at her and said…

Well done sweetheart…you've done so well…so proud of you…

Lou smiled back at me…I could see she was nervous…

I walked up to the heavy wooden doors of the hall and then knocked loudly…three times…

We then heard the noise of everyone standing within the room…

It was time…

Looking into her eyes…I then reached out and took her by the hand…a hand I held tight as I opened the doors and guided her into the room of love…of love for her…

The noise was deafening as we walked in…cheers of approval…applause…whistling…feet stamping…affirmations of love to love…

We sat down and then each peer took turns…sharing their words of hope and love for Lou…

It was very emotional…so heavy the essence of love within the room for someone who was going to be dearly missed…

Then…it was my turn…the last to affirm the woman about to leave…the woman who knew not that I loved her so. My words for her I had written in love and rhyme…written for fear of revealing my feelings with tears…

My words of farewell to Lou…the girl from the valleys of Wales…

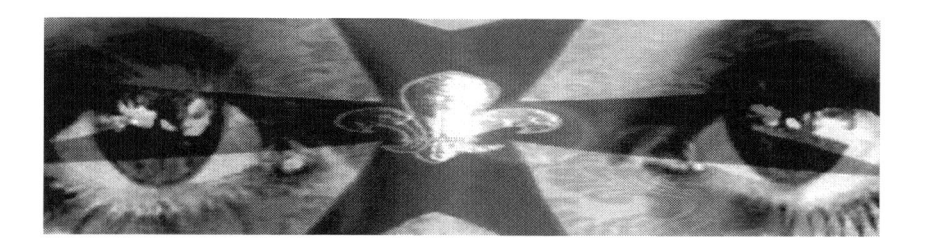

The Valley Girl, so long it rained,

Dark stormy clouds, she felt insane,

As poisoned drops, fell on her skin,

Seeped through her pores, the pain washed in.

The Valley Girl, she wandered lost,

So Beautiful, but cold like frost,

As anguish poured, forever night,

She cried alone, her tears, her plight.

The Valley Girl, a special soul,

A loving heart, it felt so cold,

Then on her knees, looked to the skies,

And what she saw was truth, not lies.

The Valley Girl, held out her hand,

Three angels smiled and helped her stand,

Serene and courage, wisdom new,

They held her close...and God did too.

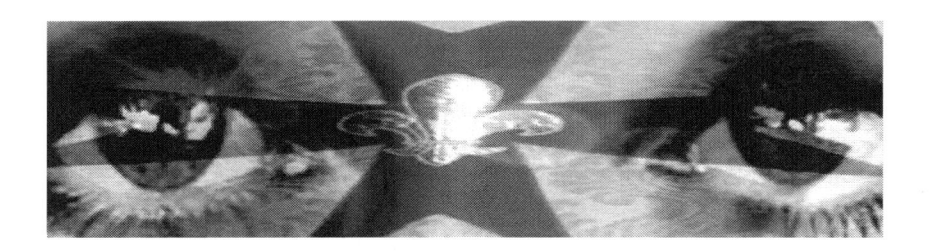

The Valley Girl, embraced by love,

Gently lifted, by high above,

A place of light, of love so pure,

It promised life, her heart a cure.

The Valley Girl, surrendered will,

Then sanity, her mind did fill,

No more alone, the angels smiled,

A mum now well, new like a child.

The Valley Girl, a soul like dew,

A love so pure, I love for you,

Your beauty's there, for all to see,

Inside my heart, you'll always be.

The Valley Girl, her name is True,

She walks with God, she walks with you,

Three Angels wait, lit like the sun,

She takes their hands...her life's begun...

Lou said goodbye…

Her goodbye took place the following day…

There were smiles and hugs and words of love from everyone as we held her close and said our farewells…

I stood nearby…not wanting to say goodbye…

Eventually…I mustered up the courage and walked towards her…

We held each other close for a short time and she said…

You've been my rock…

Then I let her go…

The Valley Girl was driven away…driven away down the long and winding driveway that welcomes the lost to *The Place of Miracles*…the same driveway that sends us back into the world…with a vision of hope…

I stood and watched her go…watched her disappear as I felt my heart break…

The Valley Girl…so beautiful and a gift to me for a short period of time…time I spent with her…time I felt inspired to do the best I could for myself and my recovery…

Lou gave me something so special…she gave me hope for myself…hope that I could have a new life…hope of a vision of something new to aspire to…

Peace in my life…a life without fear…

The girl from the valleys was now gone…another girl from the valleys remained close…so very close. *The Magdalene* was soon to reveal Her Truth to me…a Truth that would awaken my blessing of prophecy…

Happiness…

I enjoy being happy and I love to laugh…

My two months in primary care saw me awaken to so much…so much around me and within me…and it was from within me that the laughter came…

My whole life had been filled with fear…fear of the known and fear of the unknown…

So much fear carried for so long in my life…it was only by beginning to face my truth that I truly found laughter…joy from deep within…

I love to laugh and I love to see others laugh too…to help them to laugh…it's a very spiritual experience…

Laughing eyes and eyes filled with a joyous twinkle that reveals a soul for what it…something so very special…something so very happy and loving…

I love laughing and I loved finding laughter again at *The Place of Miracles*.…

Happiness in life is possible…this I now know. It isn't possible to live a life that consists only of being happy and joyous…that just isn't life…but it is possible to live a life in peace and happiness and face life on life's terms… while being at peace with one's self…and for me…that's happiness…

To aspire to happiness…to live a life of peace and joy…I had to rid myself of the past…a past soaked in fear…

Laughter aside…it was now time for me to face my fears…all fears written down…words that were to show the truth of me…

It scared me so very much…it terrified me as it dawned on me that the next Step was on its way…

It was time for my list…

Chapter Ten

Facing Fears...

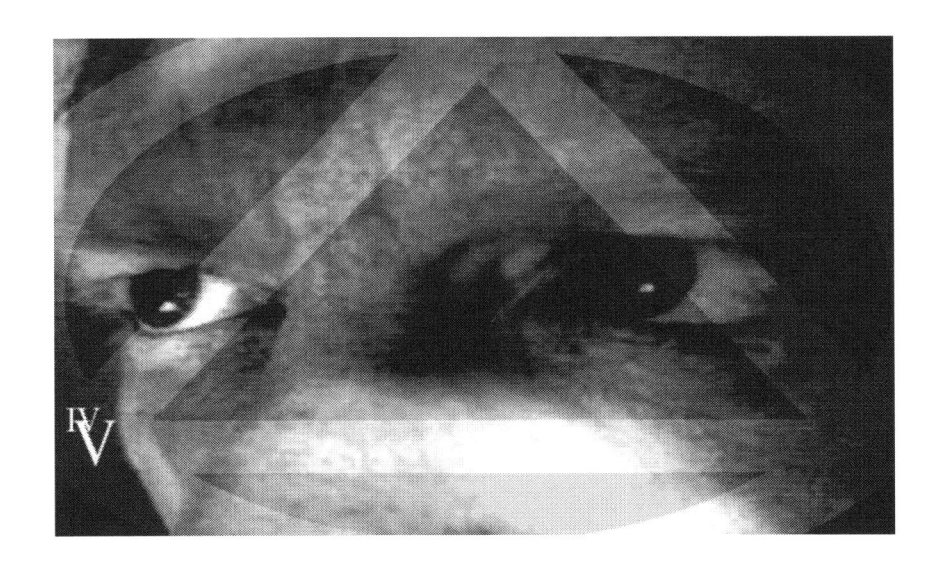

One week…

There was one week remaining for me in primary care. Soon I was to begin my secondary treatment…

Two months had almost come and gone…three months was to be the time spent in *The Garden*…the second phase of my treatment…still within the boundaries of Broadway Lodge…detached houses that sit at the foot of the two acres of beautifully manicured grounds…

The next step in my recovery beckoned…but not before my Steps Four and Five…

4. Made a searching and fearless moral inventory of ourselves…

5. Admitted to God…to ourselves…and to another human being…the exact nature of our wrongs…

Everything bad that I had done…had ever done…was to be written down and shared. I was so scared…but I was willing to be honest…

I'm a man...a human being...

A good person...a good person who's done bad things...

All of the bad things I had done...the things I had done that I thought were bad...

All of the bad things I had thought...thought of myself and of others...they were all reasons to drink...

The time had come to remove the reasons...

Searching and fearless...

Admitted...

The honest surrender of hurt to myself and to others...others who love and care for me...others who barely know me...everything and everyone...all written down and shared in a room with another human being and admitted before a power greater than myself...

My surrender to being an alcoholic had seen my awakening of spirit...beautiful and profound...joyous and uplifting...

My faith in the unseen around me had always been embraced by myself and I was willing to embark on a new life...a new path to find serenity...a peace of mind that I couldn't find in the way I saw the world and the way the world affected me...

Now it was time for another surrender...time to remove the guilt and shame for my past actions...guilt and shame and fear of what I had done in my life...

Now it was time to get honest...truly honest...so that the healing of the past could begin...a healing that would cleanse me for a future...

There were some things that I thought I would be taking to my grave...

How can I write about these things?

These were my thoughts as I prepared to take the Fourth Step…

I was willing to be honest when writing my list…but the fear consumed me. So many bad things I had done in my life…reason after reason to once again drink alcohol…

I'd made the decision upon my arrival at *The Place of Miracles* to do everything that was asked of me…I'd made a promise to myself that I would do so. The time to write my list had arrived and I was afraid. I was given one week to assemble the words…words that would reveal the nature of who I had been and what I had been….and it terrified me…

There's honesty…then there's honesty…

It was a sunny afternoon when I saw the worksheet for the first time…a paper that would guide me on what to list. Step Four…a list of headings…headings under which I was to list everything…sex…anger…pride…intolerance. The headings seemed endless…

I sat alone and gazed down at the guidelines…the headings…and as I did so…something within me…something around me seemed to be sensing to me…

It needs to be honest…everything. It must all be written down…everything. You need to do this. It has to be honest. You have nothing to fear…start writing…

My counsellor had given me the worksheets on a Thursday…then something within me told me to wait. Sunday arrived…three in the afternoon and three days in the waiting…the sense to write was overwhelming as I sensed the words...

Start writing now John…start writing now…

The writing lasted for three days…

Three days was the time it took…the time it took to look so deep within myself to find the truth of me and what I had done…

During those three days…I took a journey into the dark recesses of my past. As I wrote…I felt separated from everyone and everything around me…searching self as I searched with honesty for the words that would reveal my truth…

Three days were to pass and the words were found…three days to wait until I embraced the Fifth Step…

Moments filled with fear…moments filled with calm…moments filled with terror…then it was all written down…

For three days I found solace with my friends…my peers in *The Place of Miracles.* My time in primary care was nearing its end and I was preparing myself for the move to the secondary phase at Broadway…

But first…the Fifth…

So many peers had shared with me their experience of this Step. They all seemed to share the same stories…a feeling of relief once it was done. It's all about honesty and trust. My higher power knew my truth…all I had to do now was share it with another human being…trust in my higher power and share the honest words that would reveal the truth of me…

It needs to be honest…everything. It must all be written down…everything. You need to do this. It has to be honest. You have nothing to fear…start writing…

The time had come for me to trust in my new-found faith. Trust and faith…both the same for me and found with honesty. Threefold…a trinity that heals…

The day of my Fifth Step…

A sunny October morning saw me hold my list as I walked into a room with an elderly man…a seasoned member of the Fellowship…

We chatted for a while and there a few smiles…nervous smiles on my part…

There was a pause…then he said…

Are you ready young man?

His words felt honest and caring for me…comforting and reassuring…

Yes I'm ready…

I began to read out my list…a list of fear and resentments which had burdened me for my whole life. It lasted ninety minutes…ninety minutes during which time I shared with another human being the exact nature of my wrongs…my hurting…my fears…

I was terrified…terrified of being judged by the elderly man who sat opposite me as I read. But over and over again…I could sense something close to me saying…

Read out everything. It has to be honest. You have nothing to fear…

So I did. I shared my hurts and fears with another person and in the presence of something far greater than me…something far greater than us…

The first true act of love that I embraced was when I surrendered to being an alcoholic…

The second true act of love I ever embraced was when I rid myself of the fear and hurt of the past…when I read out my list on that sunny autumn day in *The Place of Miracles…*

My fears and resentments were done…

The man from the Fellowship asked me if I wanted to take a break. It had taken me ninety minutes to read the words that I had dreaded to share with another human being...words that shared my hurt of others...my hurt of self…

It was only once I began to read the lines that I realised just how deep I had gone when penning the words...so very deep within myself to find the truth of me. It had been so difficult to read...so difficult to share the words that had been fearlessly searched for during those three days of writing...

My list was done. By honestly sharing all of my hurt and fears with another human being and with a God of my own understanding...I'd been able to find forgiveness for the wrongs of my past and in doing so...make a fresh start to a new life…

My fears had been removed by the Grace of Truth...

A sense of relief…

Fellow peers…who had read their list…had shared with me that they'd felt a sense of relief once it was done…

In the small attic room…I rose from my chair and bid the kind old man farewell…farewell with a handshake that was honest and   grateful…

Thank you so much…

His kind blue eyes looked deep into mine…

Go well young man. You've done well…

We parted and I found myself outside the mansion…standing alone…alone and anxious as I lit a cigarette…

I couldn't understand why I was feeling irritable…it didn't make sense when others shared of a sense of peace…a sense of relief…

The day passed and my attitude and behaviour became out of character with my usual light-hearted and positive self. In a group session with fellow peers…I sniped at them and challenged their truths in a cold and callous manner…

A good friend…a fellow peer who had become like a brother to me…took me aside and asked me what was wrong? Why I was so angry? We sat together in the gardens and I shared with him that I seemed to filled with fury…with no idea as to why?

The day passed and the anger gradually subsided…

It was only to be months later that I would come to realise why I'd been so angry after reading my list. I'd been filled with fear following the reading of the truth of me…fear at the truth of what I'd once been…

Anger is based on fear…fear is the truth of anger…

My Medallion…

My Primary Care had come to an end…

Two months of hard work…eight weeks that saw me learn so much about my illness…a time of forging strong friendships with fellow peers…a blessing of time that embraced my spiritual awakening in the lecture hall…and it was in that hall where I said farewell to my peers…my friends. My final night in primary…a night that saw them share their goodbyes to me…and my farewells to them…

Now it was my turn…

Only a week had passed since standing in the hallway with Lou…now it was my turn...

I waited outside the lecture hall…nervous at what was to come…anxious that I would be the focus of attention…the attention of around thirty peers…

I am a confident man…but I struggle with affirmation…I'm a confident man with low self-esteem and self-worth...

Standing outside the hall…

I stood outside the hall…in the main corridor of the mansion…

I wasn't alone. Vincent was with me…the young man from the north who had become like a brother to me. I'd asked him to give me away…

We stood in silence in the hallway…looking at each other and exchanging smiles…with my smiles clearly showing my nervousness at what was to come. Using his nickname for me…Vincent took my hand and with a smile of love he said…

You'll be ok Guv'nor…

Vincent delivered three loud knocks. We could hear everyone stand up inside the hall. Then…my friend took my hand and he opened the doors …doors that opened to my Medallion…

The hall erupted…

The noise was deafening and I immediately became embarrassed…

Around thirty peers seemed to go wild…screaming and shouting affirmations…stamping on the wooden floor…clapping hands…whistling…and chairs being banged up and down on the floor…

I felt so humbled…I wanted to cry…

We all took our seats and the Medallion began…

The ceremony took around an hour…sixty minutes of affirmations from my peers…my friends who had shared so much with me…who I had shared so much with…

The came my turn to speak…my time to share back to everyone in the room. I shared back to every individual…from me to them…

I spoke…shared with them of how I felt…my feelings for them…

It was difficult…

It was difficult because I was so filled with emotion...of gratitude for my peers...so grateful to have spent two beautiful months at Broadway. I felt truly humbled to be with them...to be sharing my final night in Primary with them…

There was a funny little poem I'd written...then I finished with words from so very deep within me...true and honest words of how I felt for them...my friends in recovery...

We are unique. We are brothers and sisters who share the same illness. We are alcoholics...we are addicts...and no-one can ever take that away from us. We are bound together by faith in each other...faith in our higher powers...

We stand side-by-side in the trench of early recovery...awaiting the call to go over the top. One-by-one...we will take our turn and climb the ladder into No-Man's Land...Life on Life's Terms...where the Steps we have embraced will keep us safe from harm...

I regard you all as my brothers and sisters. Remember...we are special. We have shared in our darkest hours...now we share in the light of sobriety. You are my brothers and sisters and I will never forget you. I will never forget you…

I trembled as I read those words for my friends...

Primary Care was completed…Secondary awaited…

A further three months of rehabilitation in *The Place of Miracles*…away from the mansion building…houses that sit at the foot of the grounds where Angels heal. Collecting my personal belongings…I carried my bags down to where my next period of treatment would begin…

There's a lovely archway that separates the two phases of care…an archway shaped by a beautiful hedge that welcomes every new peer into *The Garden*…Secondary Care. This was to be where I would truly face myself…long and hard I would face the truth of me and what had to be done to make the changes possible…changes to the aspects of me that had caused all of the harm…

If I thought writing my list was going to fearful…well…what awaited me during the next three months was to take that fear to another level. Honesty would rid me of my fears…my fear of life…my fear of self…my fear of the known…my fear of the unknown…

I will do everything they ask of me…

Chapter Eleven

Facing Myself...

Two weeks…

For two weeks I yearned to return to the solace of Primary Care. It had been my safe haven...a place where I had felt secure...

So much had happened to me there...so much I had experienced...the place where my recovery began...the place where I'd made my new friends...the very special place where my awakening had opened my eyes to the real possibility of a life with happiness…

I missed the old mansion so much...but I got on with what needed to be done in *The Garden*...Secondary Care. My Step work had seen me complete One through Five in Primary. The surrender to being an alcoholic...coming to believe in a power far greater than me...and a willingness to live my life differently…

It made sense...

My fears and resentments had been let go with my list and now it was time to take a look at what aspects of me were causing all of the harm...the harm to myself and the harm to others…

I missed the place of my beginnings at Broadway Lodge as a new beginning dawned for me in the Garden...the beginning of a new search within me...a search to find the truth of what parts of me were defective...what parts of me had created all of the content of my list...my fears and resentments…

Now it was time to look at the core...identify those aspects of me that were causing all the harm…

To do this...I was in the right place…

The Garden was the next stage...more responsibility...more free time with self...more time to sit with myself and tale a long and hard look at me...

Secondary Care...

The secondary houses sit at the lower end of Broadway's grounds. There are five houses...with each residence housing four peers...

The only similarity with primary care is the continued daily group sessions...peers challenging peers to get to the truth...the truth of us. Honesty is a must at all times...apart from that...it's completely different...

The Step work workload is increased...additional assignments on individual character traits are many. Peers are given more responsibilities...cooking...cleaning...gardening...more free time to come and go from the unit on a daily basis...opportunities to take home leave to visit family...

Peers must also attend three Fellowship meetings a week in nearby Weston. The onus is on the peer...it's another step towards reintegration back into the world. It's all about taking responsibility...taking more action in taking responsibility for one's own life. It's a busy workload...

Two weeks…

It took me two weeks to settle into the new routine...a routine so new and a lot harder than primary care…

It had to be that way…

The weeks passed and I soon found myself becoming a part of a new group of friends in the Garden…

Once again...new faces became good friends and we all just got on with what had to be done…

The group sessions were incessant and the challenging was a lot more mature than what I was used to...more insightful regarding attitude and behaviour...more learned views on how to work the Steps in everyday life...so I learned a lot from my peers...especially those who had been in secondary for some time…

At the end of a long day...we would enjoy a cooked meal together...share about our day and even indulge in more challenging if required...it was always challenge…

It was all part of the spirit of the programme...if you had something to say...then say it...nothing to fear by being honest…

Sometimes the truth hurts...if it does...then ask yourself why? That's how the healing begins…

The healing involved a very long day. Fourteen hours of getting honest...group sessions...counselling...challenging...eating...eating and challenging...swearing...Step work...laughter...tears...more swearing...cigarettes...assignment work...screaming...more laughter...Fellowship meetings...mood swings...another tear...lights out…

It was madness...a madness where I was finding my own sanity...

The Sixth...

For me...it was all about Step Six for me in secondary...

We were entirely ready to have God remove all these defects of character...

Defects of character...aspects of me that were harmful to myself and others...aspects of me that were the foundation of my list...aspects of me that could very well cause me to drink again...

As a human being...I'm not perfect...never was...never will be...

I used to think that perfection was attainable for me...I used to think I was perfect...

No perfection for me...my defects of character were many...

Arrogant...egotistical...false pride...over-confident...narcissistic...intolerant...impatient...

So I had my list...a list that was difficult to make...but honest nonetheless...

I then held a group with fellow peers...a group during which I asked them what they thought my defects were?

Arrogant...egotistical...over-confident...people-pleaser...

My peers delivered my defects in a matter of seconds...my peers had no hesitation in sharing with me as to how they saw me. I was grateful for that...grateful yet stunned...

It had taken them seconds...

It had taken me a lot longer to find my defects...a lot longer to look deep within myself to see a true reflection of me...clear and honest. How I saw myself was not the same as how others saw me...and that was to hurt me...

Now I was fearful...fearful of the real me...

November…

Early November of that year was one of the most stressful times I've ever had to experience…

I would fall into bed at night...exhausted at what I'd been facing during the day...then awake in the morning...dreading facing another day of it…another day of me...another day of facing my defects...writing about them...sharing them with others...addressing them and working on a solution to overcome them…

A change in attitude...and so a change in behaviour...a change in attitude and behaviour and so...with hope and hard work...a change within me that would save my life…

Easier said than done...change isn't easy...change can hurt...

It was a struggle...days filled with tears and truth...tears from within me regarding the truth of me. There were some mornings when I just didn't want to get out of bed...mornings when I would lie in dread...mornings when I sensed the words…

You have to do this John...get up and do this...get up and face yourself...you need to do this…

There were so many of those dreaded mornings when I struggled to even make it to the bathroom to get ready for a new day. On each and every one of those mornings...I would have a look at a picture...a paper print of a photograph which I had pinned to a cork board above my bed…

It was a photo of a man...a man who did something great...a man whose courage...one famous day in history...inspired me to carry on during those dark mornings in secondary care…

It was my Uncle Bill...

Bill Millen...

My Uncle Bill was my gran's cousin...

It was during those early days in secondary that I was to hear of his passing...a loss that was to touch me deeply...

I'd never met the man but I'd heard of him and what he had done through stories told by my granny and my mother...

He was an extraordinary man...a quiet man...a humble man...so I was told...

Bill ended his journey in this Eden only days before I entered *The Place of Miracles*...but it was only three weeks into my secondary care that I was to find out about his passing...

It happened like this...

I was asked to give a presentation to my peers...a workshop on the third Step...the Step of Faith. I immediately thought of Bill...

It was his story I was to use as an example of faith...faith in something we cannot see...a belief in something far greater than us...

Only days after giving the workshop...I felt powerfully drawn to find an image of Bill...so I went online. It was only then that I found out he had just met his end...a peaceful end in Devon at the age of eighty-eight...

Bill's story seemed to get the attention of my peers...it also gave me the inspiration to face myself on those dark winter mornings when I dreaded getting honest about my defects of character...

A quiet man and a humble man...Bill's passing was very much online because of what he did one day in history. My uncle's peaceful end was reported all around the world...

Uncle Bill…

My Uncle Bill Millen is seen closest to the camera…with his back to the lens as he prepares to jump from the landing craft…holding his bagpipes before him. Bill was to become known as *The Mad Piper of Normandy*…

Normandy…a place so very special…so very special in the truth of *The Magdalene*…my Mother in Light. The truth of Mary was taken from those shores in the year 1311…that part of my story is still to come…as well as how my blessing of prophecy was to awaken…

Uncle Bill. His heroics on that day…6 June 1944…were to see him become legendary on the first day of the liberation of Europe. And on those dark mornings in secondary would find me looking at this picture…

If you can do that…then I can do this…

Bill's faith in something he couldn't see inspired me to face myself with my own faith…my faith in honesty. If he could face the machine gun fire of the ill will of man…armed only with his bagpipes…then I could face the truth of myself…

They landed…

They landed on beaches of Normandy and came under heavy sniper and machinegun fire. Piper Bill marched along the shoreline of Sword Beach...blasting out the tune of *Highland Laddie* as his commando mates fell around him. The Germans thought he had lost his mind...so refused to shoot him as he played in full view of their gun sights. Inspired by his heroics...the remaining commandos stormed the beach and took the enemy positions…

Blind faith…faith in something we cannot see. My uncle had faith in his mates...had faith in what they were doing...had faith in liberating the innocent from the ill will of man. That kind of courage takes faith...blind faith...

Bill's actions gave me the strength to push forward and face the truth of myself. Although I never met *The Mad Piper of Normandy* while he was here on his journey...I did hear from him one night in April 2011...words of support from the white light of Heaven…

Go well John. Go well son...

My uncle helped me so much…

What he did that day…that day of history…what he did that day was to see me through my work on myself and my defects…

Several weeks were to pass and I began to feel better about myself after embracing my truth…then embracing the changes needed to grow into a less arrogant and more tolerant man…a man now searching humility…

It was such a relief when I began to sense the changes taking place within me…a sense of peace was awakening within and around me and I began to feel so much better about myself…

The hard and honest work was paying-off…so grateful I was for the new sense of serenity that I was finding in my life…a sense serene that seemed to be holding me close…

There was still so much work to be done…but by doing so much hard work on that particular Step…I realised that I had nothing to fear about being totally honest with myself…as I was gaining faith in the outcome of being truthful…an outcome that heals…

Do the right things and the right things will happen…

These words were shared to me by a good man when I was enduring my final detox in Ipswich. So true they are…so true they are because in my experience now…the right thing is always the honest thing…the honest thing always seems to see the right outcome…

They say keep it simple…it doesn't get simpler than that…

So I was growing in secondary…still lots to do…but I could feel myself changing…becoming more aware of myself and sensing more and more that there was so much more to me. My senses were awakening and heightening as my truth removed my masks…

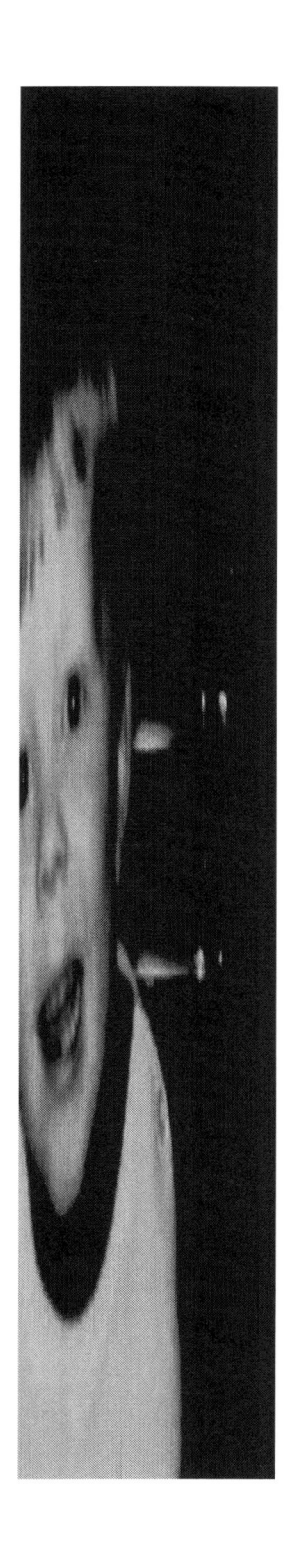

The Mask Maker

I am the Mask Maker, Mask Maker extraordinaire,

For all to see, for all to share,

Oh joyous smiles, no Fear to see,

They looked, they laughed...eyes carried me.

No masks when young, so new and pure,

A sense of awe, Hope to endure,

Beneath the sun, my Sense of all,

How could I know, what would befall?

The truth of Soul, reach out explore,

To touch of Life, please show me more,

And see I did, in darkness face,

That Life's not all in Heaven's Grace.

Light deep within, from high above,

Protect from Life, Guardian of Love,

The masks I wore, so many so,

You know me yes, you know me no.

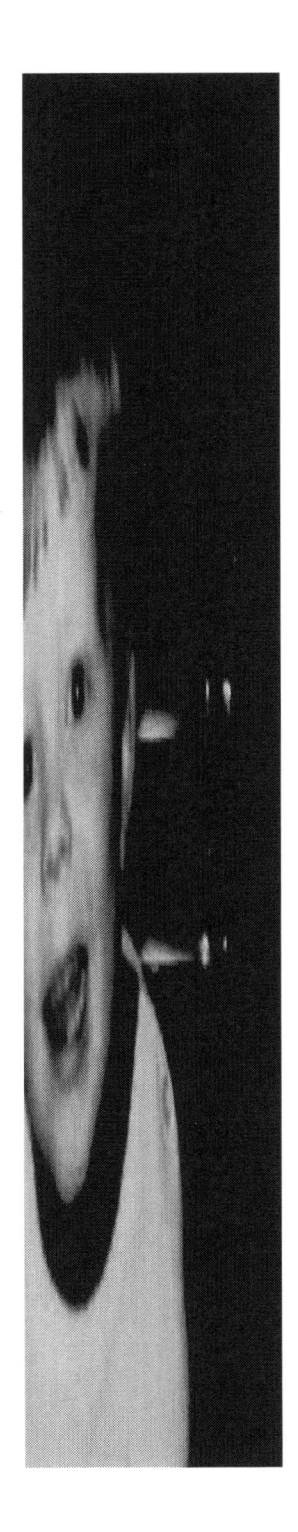

So many years, my craft my art,

The shrouds with smiles, shade scars of heart,

So many years, so now I say,

I think I'll put these masks away.

I am a man, the gentle kind,

The quiet type, with thoughtful mind,

In search of Peace, for Me in mine,

Hear whispered Fear, trust Faith Divine.

I was the Mask Maker, Mask Maker extraordinaire,

The Act is done, now me I share,

For me you see, I've always been,

An essence of. yet never seen.

I look ahead, I look within,

To see a boy, before the Sin,

Within his eyes, Hope shines like sun,

I take his hand, our time's begun…

He takes my hand, our time has come...

Sensing…

I've always been sensitive…highly sensitive…

The more I embraced honesty…the more and more I was sensing something around me…around me and so very close to me…something I could feel yet not see…

Highly sensitive and intuitive…

My whole life had seen me blessed with a gift…a gift I'd feared…

The Place of Miracles was ridding me of my fears…fears removed by embracing honesty…

Honesty…open-mindedness…willingness…

My mind had always been open to other possibilities…something within and around life that was far greater than me…so powerful and so beautiful…an essence of which I was willing to believe in…

With my new-found faith in the truth…the trinity was evolving…

I was always writing in my journal…a daily written record of what I was thinking and what I was feeling. It's been fascinating for me to look back on those words…words that didn't make sense to me then…words that make sense to me now…

I was awakening to my gift and sensing around me…I was also awakening to what would come for me…awakening to who was to come for me…

A beautiful girl with beautiful eyes…

Some say magic doesn't exist…I say if you truly believe in something magical…then it's that belief that makes the magic come alive. My awakening was elevating and I was unaware as I penned the following words…words written then that only make sense to me now…

Words written…

Some of the words written as my awakening was elevating…

We all look so different and yet we are the same. Similar essences of life on the inside…that is the real beauty of what we are…

I say what instead of who…I know that I am a person but I believe that this is an outer shell. The real me is very much on the inside and it's a sense that cannot be gauged. It can be measured by my actions and these responses are reactions to thought…but my soul is immeasurable. I see glimpses of this in others. I find the identification in a flash from a person's eyes…or an expression to which they seem unaware…

It's at these moments that I truly believe that I am blessed…for an immeasurable instant…with seeing the essence of another's soul. This is a beauty to observe and beautiful in its elation…

****

Something interesting happened to me today…

I felt…I sensed something inside me…

It told me something but didn't use words…it was a feeling. It sensed to me that I can enjoy and be happy in the moment…even though I have troubling issues to work on…

It was strange. I made me feel at peace and told me not to worry. It said that I can enjoy the moment and address the past at the same time…that I can do both. I was really odd the way that it happened…

I didn't feel scared. I felt calm and happy…like a little awakening. I think I started to giggle to myself and then carried on with my work…

****

More words written as my awakening was awakening...

I've been thinking about this for a wee while now...

I can sense she's out there...that some day we'll meet. I know she's somewhere and I'll know her when I see her. I know it will be a surprise...because I won't be looking for her and I'm really looking forward to getting to know her...really getting to know her...

I truly believe that this will happen...

Last night I dreamt of her. I was sitting in a ditch by the side of the road. It was a cobbled and cambered surface and I was sitting alongside it...in the ditch. It was dark and the starts were bright in the black sky. In the distance I could see what looked like a village...lit only by candles in windows. It looked like a scene from a fairytale and it was turquoise in colour...thanks to the moonlight...

The village looked like a village I had dreamt of ten years ago...

Sitting in the ditch...I looked to my right...I see a girl sitting beside me. She had the most beautiful green eyes I've ever seen and she was smiling at me. I felt so happy to be with her...yet neither of us said a word. We just smiled at each other and looked over at the village. I looked into her eyes again and then down at her left hand. She was wearing a stunning silver ring with a beautiful emerald embedded in the metal. I looked back into her eyes and she was still smiling at me...she made me feel so happy and complete. I reached out to touch her hand and that's when I awoke...

I would be surprised when we met...the girl in my dream. The meeting was to take place six months after these words were written in The Place of Miracles...an encounter with the most controversial woman in the history of Humankind...a woman who lived two thousand years ago...

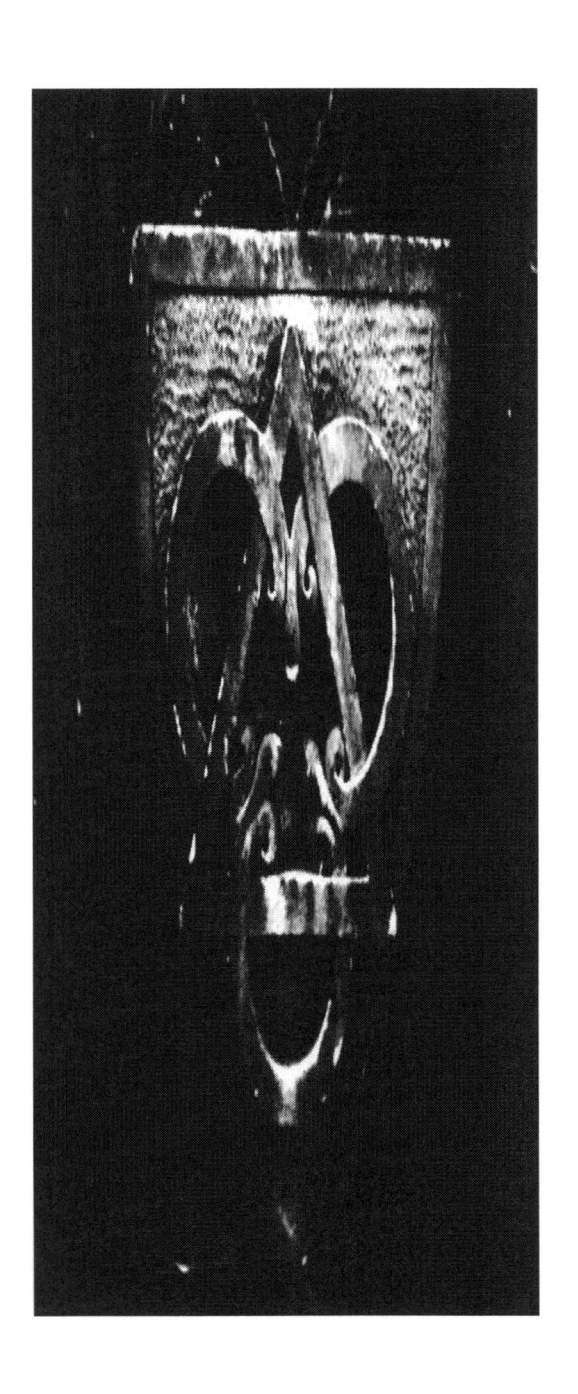

Tears softly fall
so warm in cold
This winter's grey
a day like old
I hold her close
far from their gaze
They will not take
my love this day

I hold her close
she need not fear
With brothers all
we shield her near
Tears softly fall
with Heart and Grace
We'll send them back
far from this place...

So many tears…

So many times did I break down in my counsellor's office…Sue was with me as I shed so many tears as we looked at my part in how my illness had affected the lives of others…affected me…

I broke down when I shared about how I lost Kirsty…I broke down when I shared about how I lost my best friend Marcus…I broke down when I shared of how I had once been a racist…I broke down when I shared of the time I was told to shut up as a boy during an argument my parents were having about the Holocaust…I broke down when I shared that I had an obsession with that period in history…that terrible time when man's ill will to fellow man dealt unimaginable suffering to millions across Europe…across the world. The hurt of others by others' fear had affected me terribly…

I broke down…then the rebirth began…

Sue sat with me through every tear…every tear a tiny drop of fear leaving me…every tear leaving me and being replaced with a tiny drop of healing…of understanding and forgiveness…all found through honesty. My counsellor counselled me on all that had happened and why it had happened. My morbid fascination with Europe's dark days under the fist of the ill will of Nazism was all down to one single photograph…seen at the tender age of eleven. It showed unimaginable suffering…suffering that made me feel better about where I was and who I was…a sensitive young boy who was scared. The horror that had befallen so many had provided me an escape from my own fears of life…my own fears of me. With my fears being faced…I could feel myself grow…getting stronger as I began to let it all go…let it all go and so allow the real me to come to the fore…gentle and strong…compassionate and forgiving…honest and loving…

Love and compassion...

The healing was well underway...with love and compassion...I was finding the very essence of me...finding my true self for the first time in my life...

It was working. I was working it with honesty...it was working for me...

The very essence of me seemed to lift...elevate as love showed me how to forgive myself...how love held me close and helped me to rid myself of all the guilt and shame for what I had done...for what I had thought and once believed...

Love blessed me with forgiveness...forgiveness blessed me with love for myself...love for my life...

Little did I know during that time in *The Place of Miracles*...little did I know that what was healing me was not only my hard work and the hard work of the staff...but also something beautiful and gentle that lays within The Twelve Steps...

Such a very long time ago...two thousand years...a very special message was carried by many very special people...two of whom were very gifted in their own ways. It was not to be very long before I was to meet one of them. It was not to be very long before I saw the truth of this beautiful message within the wondrous words and lines of One through Twelve. Prophecy is a blessing that sees what comes...as well as what was...

The Magdalene. Her love for me...her love for all...her message of love and forgiveness was awakening me to the truth of me and in doing so...all of the hurt from my past was being gently absolved...absolved by my hard work in embracing honesty. My truth was awakening and my truth was showing me a new me...a new me in a new life...a life which promised hope...

Life…

My life was taking a beautiful new path…a path on which I found something so special as December approached…

The evening always saw us all enjoy a meal together…sitting around the large table…laughing and eating…sometimes challenging…but mostly laughing and eating…

When a meal was done…we would all take turns to share our feelings with one another…how the day had been for us…how it made us feel…

One particular night…I found myself struggling to share. I knew I was feeling something…but had no idea what it was. So powerful was this…so overwhelming was this sense of something…that I could barely speak and became very emotional…

There were looks of concern from my friends who were sitting with me at the table…looks of genuine worry as a man not shy of words found himself speechless with emotion…struggling to share and in doing so…a few tears began to trickle down my face. By this point…my peers were really concerned…to which I said…

I'm okay…I'm okay…I just don't know what this is…I don't know what I'm feeling. It isn't bad…so powerful but I can't explain it…

Our evening meal came to an end as held hands…saying the serenity prayer together. I then went to my room where I sat alone. It was there that I awakened to what the feeling was…

Gratitude…

So powerful was this feeling that it left me humbled. Gratitude and humility…two of the most powerful feelings I've ever experienced…both in one single moment…

So grateful for life…

My life had been about fear...now the fear of life and the fear of me was ebbing away…disappearing as I began to find peace...began to find happiness…

My time at Broadway Lodge was nearing its end...but not before the festivities of Christmas on the west coast of England were to be enjoyed. So many fond memories of that time I have...so much laughter and smiles were enjoyed by myself and my friends…

We secondary peers produced a Christmas Pantomime for the peers in Primary care. We were all in it together...addicts far away from home at a time when families traditionally come together. It was the best festive season that I've ever known. The time of giving saw us give of ourselves to others like us...giving with smiles and support for one another...giving with love and care for one another as we all rallied round and made it a Christmas to remember...and remember I will for the rest of my days…

It wasn't about money or gifts...it couldn't have been because we'd all lost everything. It was about something so much more...it was about togetherness and laughter...supporting one another with hugs and smiles…

As the snow fell softly upon the seaside town of Weston-Super-Mare...I looked up at the sky of cloud and thanked Heaven for being alive...alive in such a special place with so many special people. I looked up at the snowy Heaven and thanked love for my new life…

Grant me the serenity to accept the things I cannot change…

Serenity was holding me close and I was truly happy...happy in finding the real me...at peace with being an alcoholic...my gift was Hope...

Hope...

My final few weeks saw me see a new vision of what my life could be...a life with Hope...

As a senior peer on the verge of moving back into the world...I was given my own room in House Three...

It was in this room that I would begin to experience the beginnings of being very aware that there were others near me...with me...others who loved me...others unseen...

At night I would lie in bed and simply share with them about my day...ask them for guidance...pray for them to help others who were lost to the world...

I humbly call on the essence of love all around me to be with me and give me strength to do what needs to be done. Please be close to those who love and care for me...those who I love and care for. Please help those who are lost to the world...those who I do not know...those who do not know me. Please help me to help them...please help me to see what needs to be done...Amen...

They were unseen...but I knew they were in the room with me...so very close to me...guiding me and holding me in love. I knew they were with me...I sensed them close...sense that there were four...sense that they loved me so much...

So grateful and humbled I was to know that they were with me...so honoured to have them close to me...

The essence of love unseen is what I called them...the essence of light so white. Drifting off to sleep...I felt blessed as they watched over me. Sensed but not seen...they blessed me with Strength and Hope. I would drift of to sleep...a man with no religion...a man with Truth as his Faith...a man awakening to visions from Heaven...

By the Grace of God…

By the Grace of a God of my understanding…I had reached the end of my rehabilitation…

Five months of hard work…

I'd made friends…friends for life…my life…my new life. Week after week of laughter…tears…more laughter…more tears…

Five months of embracing honesty…one profound spiritual awakening…one love found and one undeclared love lost when *The Valley Girl* departed…all Twelve Steps completed…two counsellors…nearly one hundred peers met…thousands of words written…many poems (most too rude to be included here…but will feature in a separate publication entitled *Bottoms Up!*) More hard work…one home visit…several hundred resentments…many Fellowship meetings…three main shares delivered…many main shares listened to…several peers told to leave because of dishonesty…two life stories…many Medallions attended and two final leaving celebrations of my own…

I also had a crush on a member of staff…well…three members of staff if I'm honest…but best not to elaborate on that now…

It was the most incredible experience of my life…so profoundly beautiful…that I would do it all over again…

The Place of Miracles had performed a miracle…no longer did I even contemplate picking up a drink…a non-thought that remains as I write these words…twelve months later…

More importantly…*The Place of Miracles* had guided me towards the truth of me…a loving and caring and gifted man…a gifted man who was about to experience the true extent of his gift…the gift of second sight…

Two nights…

Two nights remained for me in the Place of Miracles…

Two nights remaining as I stood outside House Three and looked across at the horizon to where the lights of Bristol twinkled in the night sky. What I was to experience at that moment...that moment on that chilly January evening...still finds me filled with emotion when I think of it. These are the words I wrote in my journal that night…not long after that moment…

The Grace of God embraced me as I looked across to the night lights above a Weston sky. Something was pulling me outwards and towards the skyline. It told me that I am ready to take the next step...the next step towards my new life out there. I can feel myself disengaging. The feeling began at around 11am . The sense is readying me for my farewells...it's time to go over the top. I suffered with the Grace of my higher power. It was always with me...always loving me. This Grace is with me now as I take the next step in my recovery. Tonight...with the Grace of a God of my understanding...I looked over towards a night light sky...as I felt the tears run down my face as I sensed the light so white say these words…

We're waiting for you in Bristol...

I said goodbye…

So many people I thanked…thanked from the bottom of my heart…

The Angels are many at *The Place of Miracles*…some unseen…many seen…

The staff gave me so much…so much that I will never be able to thank them enough for all the support they gave me…

They are the Angels who can be seen at Broadway Lodge…

It was an emotional farewell to my counsellor Sue…the woman who had guided me towards letting go of my past so that I could grow into the man I was becoming. Sue shared with me these words…

Think of yourself as a young eaglet…we are the mother eagle…we'll always be here as you're learning to fly…

No truer words spoken…the eagle was about to become a very important part in the rest of my new journey. Sue held me close and I cried…

The picture of Bill was the last thing to be packed. Looking at his image…the image of him about to jump from the landing craft. I thanked him for all the strength he had given me…

Packing Bill's picture away…I had no idea that I was packing away very special location…

Normandy…

The place where the truth of *The Magdalene* was to leave Europe in 1311…

I had no idea as I packed my things that I would meet her in three months…no idea that I was blessed with the divine gift of prophecy…

Chapter Twelve

Eyes Open...

"Liberty is the right of every human creature, as soon as he breathes the vital air; and no human law can deprive him of that right which he derives from the law of nature"

The words of John Wesley...founder of the Methodist movement in the 18th century...son of the gem on England's west coast...

Bristol...

Beautiful...welcoming...historic...my new home...

Liberty is the right of every human creature...

Words spoken amid the darkness of man's ill will towards fellow man. Bristol was built on and Bristol flourished during one of the darkest periods in the history of mankind...

The Slave Trade...

The city's unique location on the banks of the River Avon has seen it play a prominent role in marine trade for centuries...including the leading slaving port between 1730 and 1745...

Black Boy Hill...Whiteladies Road...names of places that remain from times gone by...dark times gone by...

It's believed that just over two thousand ships set sail from Bristol between 1697 and 1807...setting sail with the sole purpose of making the trip to Africa...then across the Atlantic with human cargo. The number of people is estimated at one half of a million...men...women...children...

Those days of suffering are long gone now and although the legacy of those dark times remain in dates and words...Bristol is a vibrant and welcoming city with smile and embrace replacing sorrow and chains...

The banks of the River Avon seem to reach skyward as far as the eye can see...steeples of faith planted firmly in cliffs of red stretch upward...upwards towards heaven...upwards towards God. Faith resonates in a city once darkened by the past...faith stands tall in mortar and stone as ancient places so holy lay scattered amid concrete still new. The now and the then embracing each other close...embracing me closer as my new home in recovery...liberty in my life so new. From out of the darkness that is the city's past...shines a light of hope for all...for everyone...

Freedom…

The boundaries of care were now no more…

My time at *The Place of Miracles* had come to an end and the west coast city of Bristol was to be where I would begin a new life for myself…

A haven so safe in a house in the suburbs…owned by Broadway Lodge…was where I was to accept the responsibility of caring for myself…a new home shared with three other men also in recovery…

A safe place to rest my head at night…

The past had gone…only the present was to be my focus as I looked toward laying a Fellowship foundation that would stand me true for one day at a time…

The time was January 2011 and my time had begun in Bristol…beautiful Bristol…

Fresh from the treatment centre…I felt strong and optimistic about what lay ahead for me…but I had no idea what was to very quickly begin to take place. I sensed that something very important was about to happen and that I would somehow play a part in it…but there was no way that I could have possibly anticipated what was to come for me. They say everything happens for a reason? For me…within a matter of three months…I was to find the very reason for the very existence of me…

How could I have possibly known what was awaiting me when I sensed those words on the eve of my departure from Broadway?

We're waiting for you in Bristol…

It would have been impossible to know…

The waiting was short…

What follows now…I will do my best to keep simple…

It's important that I do this because I've experienced and seen so much over the past twelve months…so simple seems best…

When I arrived at my new home in the suburbs of Bristol…I had one suitcase and several black bin bags filled with clothing. That was all I had left over from my old life…

What I did have in abundance…something of true value…was my faith in the importance of honesty…an open mind…and a willingness to believe in something far greater than me. I didn't have much in a material sense…but I had something that was much more valuable…I was alive…alive and with Hope…

And so it's with Hope that I carry this message…Her message to you…

Hope that it will help you in your life…the same hope that Her message has now given me in my life. For two thousand years Her story has lain in wait to be told…the telling of which I now carry to you. This path in life on which I now walk as taken a delicate and beautifully profound direction. For this blessing…I am truly humbled and truly grateful. For it's in Bristol where part of the greatest secret known to humankind lays hidden…a message entombed in time…a truth sought for so long…

We're waiting for you in Bristol…

How was I to know…that when I sensed those words…that I would be asked to show the world the truth of Mary Magdalene…that I would be shown where Her Truth lays in wait. I was on the verge of the greatest adventure…an adventure which was to also embrace the blessing of prophecy…

Manila comes for you…

We're waiting for you in Bristol…

Those words resonated within every part of me when I arrived in this special place on the west coast…

Living in a house with three other men in recovery…I set about   doing all of the suggested things…

The suggested things are what is recommended for someone like me to maintain a good recovery from my illness. I needed to attend Fellowship meetings. I needed to find a home group…a meeting where I would help with anything that was required…from setting-up to being responsible for the selling of literature. I needed to be willing…

I needed to find a sponsor…someone who I could share my daily life with…someone who would guide me on working the Step programme of recovery…

I needed to do voluntary work…to give something back to the community…a community which I had taken so much from during my years in active addiction…

The suggested things…

And so it was with an enthusiasm to make things right that I undertook this new journey in my life…a journey that was to become an adventure so profound that it still sometimes sees me sit and weep…gentle tears of gratitude at what I'm experiencing…what I'm being shown…

My new life began with meetings…sharing…new friends…people like me…those who suffer with the same illness as I do…those who the world considers lost…

We aren't lost…we can be found sharing with honesty all around the world…

New friends…

It didn't take me long to make many new friends…beginning with my housemates…men like me…men who once suffered terribly in addiction…

Living together and recovering together…for me…an experience so special because we're so similar…so similar in as much as we understand each other when no-one else really can…

My new housemates helped me so much to feel so welcomed in my new home…a place of safety from which I immediately began to explore my surroundings…Bristol…

Beautiful Bristol…

From the very start…I made my way into the city centre to walk the streets and attend the meetings…

Within the rooms of Alcoholics Anonymous…I was to meet so many wonderful people…people who I can now call my friends…people who I know will be my friends for the rest of my time on this incredible journey in life…

There's a saying in recovery that I hold dear…

This too shall pass…

My life of old had passed…my life of new lay before me…my life of new was guiding me towards good people…good people who had done bad things…good people who were making amends for what they had done and in doing so…were awakening as human beings…good people…

Beautiful Bristol and wonderful people…I felt blessed and I still do feel blessed…blessed with the gift of life in a city of wonder…on a journey in life that's now so wonderful…

Inspired…

Those early days were so inspirational for me and yet when I say those early days...it was only twelve months ago…

Exploring the city and doing the suggested things...I spent many hours with a close friend of mine from the treatment centre…

Tim is a man unique...a man who I consider to be my best friend in recovery...a man with an incredible talent for art and painting…a man who I admire and a man who I was fortunate enough to get to know in *The Place of Miracles...*

We spent many hours together in Bristol...sharing with each other about our new lives...new lives and so new beginnings...lots of sharing in the cafes in in our new home town…

It was during one of those coffee drinking sessions...that I shared something with him. I told Tim that I had a feeling that something very important was going to happen...something very special and that we would somehow be involved. I shared with my friend that I had no idea what it was...but I somehow knew that it was going to happen...and that we should get ready…

We're waiting for you in Bristol...

I shared with Tim those words...words which I believed were somehow sensing to me this feeling...a sense of something very important…

My parents had given me a gift of an expensive camera for my fortieth birthday. It was one of the very few items of any value that I had left in the world. I handed it to Tim that day…

I need you to take photographs of Bristol mate. I have a very strong feeling that we're going to need them. You're artistic eye is unique...please take some pictures of Bristol for me...

I began looking…

My sense that something of importance was on its way inspired me to seek an answer to something else during my first month in the house in the suburb of Kingswood…

One evening…during a conversation with one of my housemates…the local spiritualist church was mentioned…

I immediately felt a need to go to this place of faith…

As I've already mentioned…I've never been religious…but always a man who believes in something far greater than me…so with this belief…I ventured to this nearby place of light along with my housemate…

It was the Sunday evening following our discussion and it just felt right for me to be there. I felt at peace…

It was February…dark and cold on the streets of Bristol…yet within the walls of the church was a feeling of warmth and a new sense of purpose began to awaken within me…

For two months I was to attend the Sunday services…two months during which time…through the words of the mediums… I received several messages from loved ones who had ended their journeys in this Eden…

The messages from light…messages from Heaven…I knew were for me. They were unmistakably from those who knew me…those who had once loved me…those who still love me…

It was on my second Sunday visit to the church that I was to receive a message with a difference…

The difference in the message was that it came from two people in light…two people in Heaven…two people who I didn't know…

The man and the woman...

The second Sunday visit to the place of faith saw me once again   sitting in the back of the church with my housemate...

Once again...the service began with hymns and readings...song and words of hope. The guest medium that evening was a lovely woman...a woman called Sharon and someone who I was to later share my experiences with...

With the songs of faith and words of hope at an end...Sharon stood before the modestly numbered congregation and began carrying the messages from light...the messages of hope...to those who sat before her...

Loved ones and friends...lovers and family...those now in the light so white offered words and wisdom to those they left behind...to those they will see again...

The service was almost at an end when Sharon looked over the heads that sat before me. Looking straight at me...she said...

The gentleman at the back...can I come to you?

I replied *Yes* and she continued...

There's a very strong feminine essence around you. You see the world through two sets of eyes. You see the world through the eyes of a man as well as the eyes of a woman...and this is very rare...

Now I see a man and a woman standing before you. They're saying that it's a privilege to be working with you. They like the way you think...

They're standing before you...now they're presenting you with something... they're laying it before you...it's a child...a baby...

There's something else. Now they're presenting God before you...

I was presented with God in February 2011…

The God word bothered me. Not religious now…not religious then…I walked away from the church on that cold and dark winter's night feeling confused at what I'd been told. The streets were wet with rain from the Heavens as I made my way home…street lamps lighting my path as I asked myself the same questions over and over again…

Why are they showing me God? I'm not religious. Why am I being shown God?

The events that followed in the months to come can only be described as profound…a word I don't like to use now as what I experience isn't profound to me anymore…since these experiences are now part of my daily life…visions from Heaven…

The visions were to begin several weeks after God was presented to me in the warmth of that small place of Faith in the suburbs of Bristol…a city of beauty on England's west coast…

It all seemed to come very naturally to me and it didn't scare me. Memories of when I was a young boy began to return…memories of when I was alone…I would whisper nearly silent words to what I must have known was around and within me…

Please don't let me see…please…please…I don't want to see…

It was becoming clear. By embracing the importance of honesty in my life…many fears had been removed…including my lifelong fear of my blessing from Heaven…

It all seemed to happen so very quickly for me…to me…as my senses became more and more heightened as the days passed…as the hours passed…to the point where I started to see the unseen in my new home in the presence of my new housemates…

I was seeing the unseen…

I began learning how to meditate. These meditations were to take place in the same church where I'd been presented with God. They came invaluable in my understanding of my gift...as well as the evolving of my blessing…

It was after one such evening of meditation when I had my first clairvoyant experience involving another person. My housemate Ian and me were talking in the kitchen upon my return from the church. My friend was to help me so much in those early days in my new home in Bristol. He also embraces open-mindedness...so was willing to listen to me when I needed to share with someone about what I was experiencing during those early days of the awakening of my gift...

So we were chatting in the kitchen...when all of a sudden...I began to see objects appear before him. I quickly explained what was happening and asked him if it was ok for me to share with him what I was experiencing...what I was seeing appear before my very eyes. Ian said…

Yes...no problem mate. What are you seeing?

My friend stood in silence as I shared...

There's stuff appearing right in front of you Ian. I'm seeing two bicycles...a coloured beach ball...an empty bird cage with the little door wide open. Now I'm seeing silver balls. They look like the kind used in that game...the game they call boules?

Ian just stood still and stared straight at me for a short while...looking puzzled...then looking pleasantly surprised. Then he said…

Everything you've described...everything...is in the entrance hall to my house...a house 100 miles away!

My blessing was elevating and it was elevating quickly…

The story of what was to come for me from that point until now is a story that comes in the second of this trilogy…*The Man With Smiles*…

My experience was to go beyond profound…an experience that was to see me stunned and on my knees on more than one occasion…humbled and in awe on so many others…

I've seen so much from the unseen over the past eighteen months I've been shown that there's still so much more to come for me. These visions were to show me details of places I knew nothing of…places I'd never been to. Yet these places unknown seemed known to me…

I really struggled with it all at times…times when I thought I was losing my mind. There were times when I thought about asking for help…a professional insight into some kind of mental delusion. But during these times I held on tightly to my trust in my faith…a faith that had awakened within and around me on that beautiful late summer's day in 2010 in the treatment centre on England's west coast…

My faith is the truth. And the truth now sees me a man with peace of mind and freedom from a terrible illness. That can only be a good thing…

This solace I now find in my life has now also helped those who I love to also find peace of mind. Those who love and care for me…those who I love and care for…now see me happy in my new life…a man with new found hope…a man with smiles…

So something beautiful and precious has happened not only for me…but for others too…and that's what blesses me with the smiles I have today…

Bu not all I see is worthy of a smile. I was to see so much and not all was or is good…

On 24 September 2012...the following words appeared before me...

Witness comes for you...

I sent myself a text...

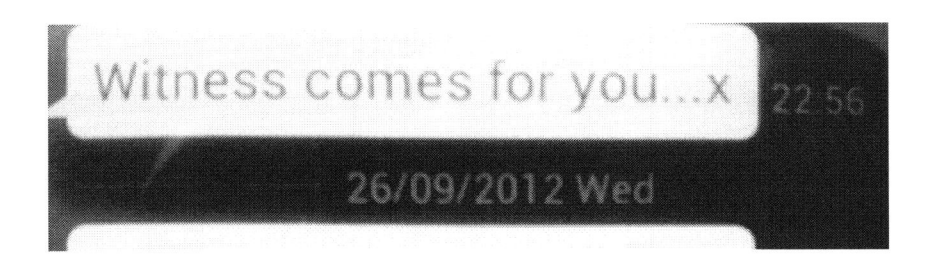

Two days later...on 26 September 2012...Iran unveiled a new "indigenous" long-range unmanned drone capable of flying over most of the Middle East. The drone is capable of carrying bombs and missiles. Iran named the drone...Shahed...

Shahed means Witness...

The Man With Smiles will reveal what I was to see and what I was to experience before this gift was to elevate to what it was to become...as well as details of the Truth a woman so very special...a woman who lived so long ago...

It's written she came from a far away place. It's written she came from Magdala...

A lot was to happen before I saw that Truth...

The sun was shining…

It was a sunny spring day in 2011. My senses were heightening and my blessing of second sight was elevating so quickly…

I was standing alone in the kitchen of my new home in Bristol…a safe haven for my new life that awaited me…

I knew I was blessed…but I had no idea what my blessing was…

There was no-one else in the house when I looked upward and asked a simple question to the Heavens above…

What am I?

A single word appeared before me…

SEER

To be continued...

John Thomson is currently living in Bristol, England.

It's this west coast where he began his recovery from alcohol addiction...a recovery that sees him nearly two years sober. Honesty is the foundation of his new life...his abstinence...his Faith. John's awakening of spirit took place in a treatment centre for addiction in September 2010 and has continued to be profound ever since...with visions taking place daily.

John was born into an ordinary working class family near the River Clyde in Glasgow in 1967.

The eldest of three children...John grew up in a loving home in Southern Africa...a country where he was also exposed to the horrors of extreme violence during the Apartheid era. He returned to Scotland at the age of twenty-five and began a long and successful career in television broadcasting. A respected journalist and programme maker...he was to eventually produce and direct the world's longest-running sports programme of its time. His illness...the illness of alcoholism...eventually forced him to stand down from his position and he spent many years in the chaos of his illness.

John's recovery now sees him embrace the importance of Honesty in his life...a truth he finds within the unique Twelve Step programme of recovery...a truth that has awakened his experience of visions...

24989825R00116

Printed in Poland
by Amazon Fulfillment
Poland Sp. z o.o., Wrocław